Here's what people are saying

What Color Is Your Brain?

This book changed my life. I use the concepts every day to communicate more effectively with the people around me at work and at home!

Mary Ellen Thielemann, Vice President, Retail banking

This book is a gem! At last, an easy-to-read, useful-right-now, non-judgmental resource at your fingertips. Sheila Glazov has made the complicated simple and the confusing easy to understand.

Kevin E. O'Connor, CSP, Author, *Present Like a Pro: A Field Guide to Mastering the Art of Business, Professional, and Public Speaking*

Sheila Glazov's What Color Is Your Brain? *can help us be more aware and comfortable in our critical communications, understand our motivations, how we impact others, and build successful business and personal relationships.*

Hedy Ratner, Co-President, Women's Business Development Center

As a trial judge, I found Sheila Glazov's latest book, What Color Is Your Brain?, *to be of great assistance in my ability to ascertain the fairness and impartiality of prospective jurors.*

Judge Richard J. Elrod, Circuit Court of Cook County, Illinois

Sheila's style is easy to understand and her examples are profound. An exceptional resource for professionals, partners, and parents.

Cecelia "Fi" Mazanke, Founder, Direct Connect Coaching

I wish I had What Color Is Your Brain? *as a guide over these last several decades. I look forward to having this book help me better navigate the remaining voyage. Sheila Glazov has taken a topic of importance to every single person in every single setting and made it understandable and usable.*

Michael F. Epstein, MD, Executive VP and Chief Operating Officer, Beth Israel Deaconess Medical Center

Sheila Glazov's conceptualization of personality styles is brilliant. It is a helpful tool for anyone working to improve life functioning. I have successfully utilized her practical and fun ideas in my family therapy practice and recommend them to others.

Ellen Sherman, PhD, LMFT

I wasn't able to be as effective a leader until I knew what color my brain was. I've gained tremendous self-awareness through reading this book. Now, I understand what makes people tick. The result...better communication and motivation... increased sales!

Mitch Bloom, Division Manager of Vector Marketing and Cutco Cutlery

Identifying each person's color traits achieves the best from everyone! What Color Is Your Brain? *is an extraordinarily creative method. You can communicate with each individual, while working within a team system and keeping the goal in mind.*

Joni Cotten, Coach, U.S. Women's Curling Team, 2002 Winter Olympics

Invaluable! The concept of Brain Colors is readily grasped and easily remembered. We like to use Sheila's concept with new staff and interns. It's helpful and fun.

Maureen Manning-Rosenfeld, MS, LCPC, CDVP, CPAIP, Director of Client Services, Community Crisis Center

I recommend Sheila Glazov's book to all who are trying to figure out the characters in their lives. What Color Is Your Brain? *offers a universal language for all ages to enjoy and fresh ideas you can instantly apply.*

Carol Owens Campbell, Co-author of *Views from a Pier*

A great tool! The colors system is easy to understand and employ, and offers readers incredible insight into changing office dynamics.

Sue Masaracchia-Roberts, Public Relations Manager, Quill Corporation

What Color Is Your Brain? *creates an ideal environment for academic and social success, and prepares children for lifelong learning and achievement beyond the class-room.*

Michelle Bracken, SLP, Speech Pathologist/Special Education for 35 years

What Color Is

Your Brain?

A Fun and Fascinating Approach to Understanding Yourself and Others

What Color Is

Your Brain?

A Fun and Fascinating Approach to Understanding Yourself and Others

Sheila N. Glazov

INCORPORATED

Delivering the best in health care information and education worldwide

| www.whatcolorisyourbrain.com |

ISBN: 978-1-55642-807-4

Copyright © 2008 by Sheila N. Glazov

Library of Congress Cataloging-in-Publication Data

Glazov, Sheila

What color is your brain? : a fun and fascinating approach to understanding yourself and others / Sheila N. Glazov.

p. cm.

Includes bibliographical references and index.

ISBN-13: 978-1-55642-807-4 (alk. paper)

ISBN-10: 1-55642-807-3 (alk. paper)

1. Typology (Psychology) 2. Myers-Briggs Type Indicator. 3. Color--Psychological aspects. I. Title.

BF698.3.G63 2007

155.2'64--dc22

2007017108

Published by: SLACK Incorporated
6900 Grove Road
Thorofare, NJ 08086 USA
Telephone: 856-848-1000
Fax: 856-853-5991
www.slackbooks.com

Printed in the United States of America.

Last digit is print number: 10

Dedication

To my mother and mentor, Sylvia Newman: I am grateful for her "Yellow Brainer gifts" of tenacity, creative style, and "rependability."

To my father and teacher, Alexander I. Newman: I am grateful for his "Green Brainer gifts" of commitment, scholarship, and "tzedaka."

To my husband and partner, Jordan: I am thankful for your "Blue Brainer gifts" of "AMLF" love, truthfulness, encouragement, and generosity.

To my friend and publisher, John Bond: I am appreciative of your "Orange Brainer gifts" of enthusiasm and a "grand adventure."

Contents

Dedication...vii

Acknowledgments xi

Introduction..xiii

Section I: Brain Color Concepts

Chapter 1:   The "No Right or Wrong Answer" Brain Color Quiz 3

Chapter 2:   Recognize Your Strengths and Perspectives 7

Chapter 3:   Appreciate Our Differences.................................... 13

Chapter 4:   Understanding Your Color Combinations..................... 21

Chapter 5:   How Other Colors See You 29

Chapter 6:   Thrive in Ideal Conditions.................................... 39

            Section I: Brain Color Concepts Summary 45

Section II: Personal Brain Color Connections

Chapter 7:   Your Romantic Relationships.............................. 49

Chapter 8:   Your Relationships With Co-Workers................... 59

Chapter 9:   Your Relationships With Family Members and Friends.. 69

Chapter 10: Your Relationships With Children 77

            Section II: Brain Color Connections Summary 85

Section III: Brain Color Communication

Chapter 11: Speak Fluent Brain Color 89

Chapter 12: Connect With Others and Build Rapport..................... 97

Chapter 13: No-Brainer Conflict Resolution 105

Chapter 14: You Can Change Your Brain Color 111

Chapter 15: Effective Decision Making 117

Chapter 16: Celebrate Hassle-Free Holidays........................ 123

Chapter 17: Helpful Clues and Quotes 131

            Section III: Brain Color Communication Summary......... 135

Chapter 18: Epilogue 139

Bibliography... 143

continued

Index.. 147
An Interview With the Author... 153
About the Author... 158

Charts Index

The "No Right or Wrong Answer" Brain Color Quiz 5
My Brain Strengths and Perspective 8
How Others See Your Brain Colors... 32
My Romantic Brain Perspective 52
Co-Worker Brain Color Frustrations.. 61
Perspective of Bosses, Leaders, and/or Managers 62
Family Member and Friend Perspective 72
Student and Adult Brain Color Statistics................................... 77
Child Perspective... 80
No-Brainer Conflict Resolution 107
Brain Color Effective Decision Making.................................. 119
Celebrate Hassle-Free Holidays 124

Acknowledgments

My Orange Brain loves a challenge. However, my Blue Brain found this section of the book the most challenging. It was difficult to put into words how much I appreciate my husband, children, grandchildren, family members, friends, and colleagues. I am thankful for their generosity and I value their copious Brain Color attributes and abilities, which helped to make this book a reality.

My Yellow Brain organized each person according to how I thought his or her Brain Color assisted me, which is not necessarily how they see themselves. To be fair, my Green Brain listed everyone's name in alphabetical order.

To each of you who offered me your "praiseworthy gifts" of love, friendship, encouragement, and/or knowledge, my gratitude is more than tongue can tell!

Thank you from the bottom of my Blue Heart!

Yellow Brainers

Linda Baker, John Bond, Beverly Berman, Michelle Bracken, Carol Campbell, John Carter, Martha Christens, Maureen Cipriano, Michele Clerici, Frances Cornacchiul, Miss Dottie and Miss Cohen, Joan Fessler, Michelle Gatt, Anne Hildebrand, Holly Lampier, Sue Lewis, Tina Meeke, Carol Pape, Diane Pryde, Allyson Sachs, Kim Shigo, Elaine Siegel, Rob Smentek, Michelle Lanter Smith, Penelope Steiner, and Debra Toulson.

Blue Brainers

Barrington Area Professional Women, Troby Brockman, John DeBerry, Lori Dony, Sharon Edwards, Marilyn Elrod, Rob Esgro, D.N. Evans, Ashton Beau Glazov, Kelly Glazov, Sheryl Glazov, Yasmin Glazov, John Guarrine, Doug Gustafson, Hawthorn Woods Women's Club, Raymond Hinkle, Rosanne Hitchcock, Mary Ann Kolker, Jody Lewis, Alison Glazov Liguori, Olivia Mellan, Pam Purcell, Dr. Jane Richards, Michael P. Scott, Helene Shore Schwartz, Denise Blum Sepos, Doris Shriebman, and Cindi Waller.

GREEN BRAINERS

Gordon Alper, Caryn Amster, Bill Amster, John Bracken, John Campbell, Peter Elsner, Jordan Glazov, Joshua Glazov, Janene Harris, Bob Mazanke, Mary Merz, Ken Neubauer, and Pavlin Panayotov.

ORANGE BRAINERS

Sue Dobbe, Rob Esgro, Theresa Fenske, Noah Glazov, Toby Harris, Evelyn Hopkins, Amy Margolin, Peter Slack, Alan Smollen, Carolyn Swan, and Sandi Washer.

Thank you for purchasing my book. Ten percent of the royalties from the sale of *What Color Is Your Brain?* will be allocated to the Juvenile Diabetes Research Foundation (JDRF) to help my son, Joshua, and the other adults, children, and their families who deal with the challenges of diabetes.

Introduction

Would you like to "Work Smarter, Live Better, Love More and Laugh Often?" If you answered "Yes!" you are about to learn how, as you discover your Brain Color.

The **What Color Is Your Brain?**® (**WCIYB**) method is fun and fascinating. It also is a remarkably fresh approach and powerfully simple answer to what makes your co-workers, romantic partners, children, friends and family members tick!

WCIYB will help reduce the frustration and complication in your business life and personal relationships and improve your own and others' ability to:

1. Understand and value your personality type
2. Communicate effectively with others
3. Work more collaboratively with co-workers
4. Keep your energy up and your stress down
5. Decrease the hassles and increase the harmony in the workplace and at home

I assure you that learning **WCIYB** will be effortless, educational and enlightening. The practical applications can be implemented immediately to resolve conflicts quickly, enhance your job performance and build cooperative interaction with others.

"I've been trying to train my staff about customer service and how to understand people; I just didn't know there were colors to help me do it." A color-filled comment from a hospital supervisor.

Originally, I developed the **What Color Is Your Brain?**® workshops as an introduction for my strategic planning/creative problem solving workshops. I wanted to create a non-judgmental environment that eliminated criticism and enhanced appreciation for each individual's ideas.

The foundation for **WCIYB** is the Myers-Briggs Type Indicator or MBTI®, a well-respected self-reporting assessment tool. Isabel Briggs Myers and Katharine Cook Briggs developed the MBTI® in 1942, based on Carl Jung's four personality functions: Sensing, Thinking, Intuiting, and Feeling. They used 16 letter combinations to identify personality traits. I believe the MBTI® and other similar personality assessments offer valuable and valid information within a specific business organization, work environment, or career. However, their use of a series of letters, terms, and symbols are too confusing for children and often too complicated for most adults to remember.

"We're always looking for a way to connect, to relate, to get into someone else's head to understand how they're thinking. Colors really make much more sense than the Myers-Briggs terminology; much easier and a much more 'positive' way of identifying personality types, and colors don't label anyone in a way that one might find offensive. I like your entire approach —all very upbeat, and accepting and forgiving of 'other colors' quirkiness," a sales professional told me after she participated in a workshop and read my book.

Individuals quickly and positively respond to **WCIYB**, because the methodology:

- Uses only four colors to identify personality types
- Does not label people or put them in only one category
- Is a common language for adults and children to easily understand
- Is a bridge to connect the workplace, home, school, and community

If the title "**What Color Is Your Brain?®**" piqued your interest, I'm not surprised. We are naturally and socially inquisitive about ourselves and others. The abundance of television and radio programs, websites, magazines and social networking sites demonstrates and confirms the curiosity and fascination individuals have about each other.

The essence of my book and workshops is to help adults and children recognize and bring out the best in themselves and others. The **WCIYB** personality profile explains why your perspective differs from or is similar to the viewpoints of others. As an "instant personality decoder," it will help you decipher your unique characteristics and solve the puzzling traits and talents of others who impact your daily thoughts and actions.

To determine your personality type as a Blue, Yellow, Green or Orange Brain individual, begin reading with Chapter 1, *The "No Right or Wrong Answer" Brain Quiz,* followed by Chapter 2, *Recognize Your Brain Color Strengths and Perspectives.* Then enjoy reading, in any order that suits your Brain Color personality, the other chapters that contain detailed Brain Color content, research charts, personal anecdotes, quotes and innovative problem-solving techniques.

I encourage you to use **WCIYB** as a reference book. Keep it on your desk, in your briefcase or at the kitchen table for easier conflict resolutions, fascinating revelations and lively conversations. Soon you will be confidently speaking fluent Brain Color and translating the perplexing or predictable behavior and idiosyncrasies of the diverse personality types in your life.

Enjoy your Brain Color Adventure and Best Wishes for a Happy "Brainday"!

Sheila Glazov

SECTION I

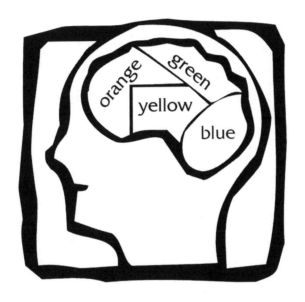

BRAIN COLOR CONCEPTS

The "No Right or Wrong Answer" Brain Color Quiz

The *"No Right or Wrong Answer" Brain Color Quiz* is a simplified personality profile that will provide you with a visual tool to analyze your characteristics and a method to recognize your attributes and abilities.

Recently, a senior staff pre-admissions testing nurse told me, "When some of my colleagues and I go on a break, I enjoy sharing the Brain Color information with them. It starts out as a form of relaxation and entertainment. 'What color is my brain? Is this a question and answer quiz?' people ask, as they look over my shoulder at the **What Color Is Your Brain?** website. I tell them it's a no-brainer. There is no right or wrong color. It's another facet of ourselves. Our personalities reflect the various colors of our brain. Before you know it, you have absorbed the information to deal with others in a more understanding and accepting manner. I think it is kinder to refer to someone by their Brain Color, rather than as an "anal retentive personality"!

The Brain Color Quiz consists of word lists and fill-in sentences. The numerical values from this process will give you a synopsis of your Brain Colors.

Six tips to remember while determining your Brain Color:

1. There are **no right or wrong answers,** *only* what is accurate about you.

2. Your Brain Colors may be different in your personal or professional life. Decide ahead of time which perspective of your life the words or sentences describe.

3. If you think two or more words in a row are of equal value, remember your perspective. Is it your personal or professional life? Or, try the following sentence:

4. In my professional (or personal) life, I am _____.

5. This is not a "**wanna be**" quiz. It does not determine *who you want to be*; it determines who you *are* at this time.

6. If you are reading this with another individual, please do not have him or her help you. The purpose of this quiz is for *you* to confirm your own Brain Color. How you see yourself may not be how others see you. According to Rita Carter, author of *Mapping The Mind*, "By the time we are adults, our mental landscapes are so individual that no two of us will see anything in quite the same way."

7. **Enjoy yourself!** The Brain Color quiz is informative and fun! In fact, it has been the entertainment for bridal showers, holiday gatherings, dinner parties, and investment club meetings.

Directions

- Read the **4** words and phrases horizontally → across each row on the page.

- Decide which word in each row describes you: Most = **4**; Not as much = **3**; Not too much = **2**; and Least = **1**.

- Rank each characteristic in the row across → using 4, 3, 2, 1 **only once** (4 = the **greatest value** and 1 = **least value** to you).

- After you have completed **all** the rows →, **vertically** add **all** the numbers in **each** of the 4 columns down ↓ to calculate your **TOTALS**.

- Record the **TOTAL** number for your A, B, C, and D columns in the appropriate **TOTAL** spaces at the bottom of the page.

- If two of your **TOTALS** were numerically equal, that is *not* unusual.

THE "NO RIGHT OR WRONG ANSWER"
BRAIN COLOR QUIZ

A	B	C	D
__ Organized	__ Creative	__ Independent	__ Enthusiastic
__ Punctual	__ Communicative	__ Curious	__ Fun-Loving
__ Detailed	__ Flexible	__ Composed	__ Competitive
__ Responsible	__ Caring	__ Analytical	__ Resourceful
__ Committed	__ Sensitive	__ Contemplative	__ Courageous
__ Careful	__ Cooperative	__ Technical	__ Energetic
__ Accountable	__ Affectionate	__ Autonomous	__ Adventurous
__ Respectful	__ Authentic	__ Competent	__ Generous
__ Predictable	__ Nurturing	__ Investigative	__ Spontaneous

When making decisions, I like to:

__ Have a plan	__ Talk to others	__ Gather all facts	__ Trust instincts

When working with others, I see myself as a:

__ Coach	__ Team player	__ Problem solver	__ Trouble shooter

I am most comfortable and thrive in an environment that supports my sense of:

__ Stability	__ Harmony	__ Privacy	__ Freedom

___ A – TOTAL	___ B – TOTAL	___ C – TOTAL	___ D – TOTAL

RECOGNIZE YOUR STRENGTHS AND PERSPECTIVES

Wouldn't it be nice to practice
This fine way of thinking too;
You know something good about me,
I know something good about you!
—Anonymous

You Are a Gem

Someone might describe you as a gem because he or she knows something good about you. We often use the word "gem" to describe an individual who is esteemed or valued.

To help people understand **WCIYB**, I ask them to think of themselves as multifaceted gemstone-quality people. I have found that people can easily connect to the metaphor visually, emotionally, culturally, and/or historically. Gemologists say that gemstones have their own personalities and are valued most for the brilliance of their color. Just like a gemstone, we value others and are attracted to the best features of their personalities.

Your Best Features

A gemstone is faceted to show off its best features. On the next few pages, match your **A, B, C, and D TOTALS** to each of the four Brain Color Strengths and Perspectives Charts to discover the best features of your personality.

You may find it helpful read about your Brain Colors according to their numerical sequence. Read the **A, B, C, or D TOTAL** that ranked highest

continued on page 10

A—MY YELLOW BRAIN STRENGTHS & PERSPECTIVE

I SEE MYSELF AS: Dependable, punctual, & responsible
I AM NATURALLY: Respectful & concerned
I VALUE: Traditions & stability
MY ATTITUDE IS: Strong sense of right & wrong
MY PRIORITIES ARE: Organization & accountability
IN THE WORKPLACE I AM: Prepared, committed, & detailed
IN MY PERSONAL RELATIONSHIPS I AM: Practical & serious
AS A CHILD I WAS: "The Model Student"
OTHERS MAY SEE ME AS: Predictable, inflexible, & controlling
I DEAL WITH CHANGE BY: Developing a plan to implement change
MY STRESS FACTOR IS: Dealing with disorganization
WHEN I AM FRUSTRATED: I can become anxious & worry
TO ENCOURAGE MY SELF-CONFIDENCE: Acknowledge my loyalty

B—MY BLUE BRAIN STRENGTHS & PERSPECTIVE

I SEE MYSELF AS: Helpful, creative, & communicative
I AM NATURALLY: Affectionate, flexible, & nurturing
I VALUE: Trustworthiness & empathy
MY ATTITUDE IS: Encouraging & compassionate
MY PRIORITIES ARE: Harmony & hugs
IN THE WORKPLACE I AM: Motivational, inspiring, & interactive
IN MY PERSONAL RELATIONSHIPS I AM: Thoughtful & romantic
AS A CHILD I WAS: Cooperative & imaginative
OTHERS MAY SEE ME AS: Overly emotional, talkative, & naive
I DEAL WITH CHANGE BY: Asking myself how the change would feel
MY STRESS FACTOR IS: Lack of cooperation
WHEN I AM FRUSTRATED: I can become depressed & passive resistant
TO ENCOURAGE MY SELF-CONFIDENCE: Acknowledge my compassion

C—MY GREEN BRAIN STRENGTHS & PERSPECTIVE

I SEE MYSELF AS: Logical, intelligent, & composed

I AM NATURALLY: A nonconformist & visionary

I VALUE: Knowledge & efficiency

MY ATTITUDE IS: Be self-sufficient & fair

MY PRIORITIES ARE: Independence & privacy

IN THE WORKPLACE I AM: Knowledgeable about the latest technology

IN MY PERSONAL RELATIONSHIPS I AM: Sensitive, but uneasy with emotions

AS A CHILD I WAS: Curious & mentally focused

OTHERS MAY SEE ME AS: Factual, insensitive, & intimidating

WHEN DEALING WITH CHANGE: I take time to process my thoughts

MY STRESS FACTOR IS: Coping with incompetency

WHEN I AM FRUSTRATED: I withdraw and can become indecisive

TO ENCOURAGE MY SELF-CONFIDENCE: Acknowledge my competency

 D—MY ORANGE BRAIN STRENGTHS & PERSPECTIVE

I SEE MYSELF AS: Dynamic, generous, & spontaneous

I AM NATURALLY: A negotiator & troubleshooter

I VALUE: Adventure & resourcefulness

MY ATTITUDE IS: Enthusiastic & courageous

MY PRIORITIES ARE: Freedom & fun

IN THE WORKPLACE I AM: Entrepreneurial & competitive

IN MY PERSONAL RELATIONSHIPS I AM: Energetic

AS A CHILD I WAS: Entertaining & impulsive

OTHERS MAY SEE ME AS: Disorganized, resistant, & irresponsible

I DEAL WITH CHANGE BY: Embracing and enjoying new opportunities

MY STRESS FACTOR IS: Someone else's rules or directions

WHEN I AM FRUSTRATED: I "drop out" physically or mentally

TO ENCOURAGE MY SELF-CONFIDENCE: Acknowledge my generosity

continued from page 7

for you first, and the one you ranked lowest last. You will discover most of your characteristics under description that you ranked the **highest**.

If two of your **totals** were numerically equal, that is not unusual. It indicates similar strengths and perspectives in those Brain Colors.

It is normal to recognize a **few** of your characteristics in the other Brain Colors Strengths and Perspectives descriptions. The other Strengths and Perspectives descriptions will also offer you insight into other people's best features.

> *"When we seek to discover the best in others, we somehow bring*
> *out the best in ourselves."*
> —Author, William Arthur Ward

Your Best Perspectives

While you were identifying your Brain Color strengths and perspectives did you think,

- "This described me to a T."
- "I'm a _____ and my husband is _____."
- "My boss is _____."
- "My kids are _____."

Before You Read More

- The term "brainers" describes or refers to individuals and their Brain Colors.
- For consistency, the sequence of the Brain Colors is as follows throughout the book: Yellow, Blue, Green, Orange. The exceptions are Chapter 10 and Chapter 12. The Brain Color sequence does not signify a preference for any particular Brain Color or its characteristics.

APPRECIATE OUR DIFFERENCES

"There is a sense of our characters caring for each other and respecting each other. A positive feeling. A positive view of life. That's the key to everything we do."
—Jim Henson, creator of the Muppets

A Positive View of Life

The positive sense of your character and your self-confidence is influenced by your values and your feelings of contentment. When you are self-confident, you have the ability to feel acceptance, self-worth, capability, empowerment, respect for yourself and others, and to solve problems effectively.

Your interaction with the other Brain Colors at home, work, or school and in your cultural community influences your positive view of life. Misunderstandings between people often are a result of not appreciating another individual's unique personality traits.

WCIYB will help you:

- recognize how other people's personalities affect you.
- value what is meaningful, relevant, and significant about each personality type.

An Explanation, Not an Excuse!

WCIYB is *not* about tolerance. Tolerance can be defined as: 1. A fair and objective attitude, 2. The act of enduring or putting up with.

I think most of us would like others to have a fair and objective attitude towards us, but not a sense of tolerance. By definition, others would endure or just "put up" with us.

WCIYB is about appreciation. I want to offer you an opportunity to learn a "color-filled" appreciation of yourself and others, and to teach you how to recognize and understand the harmonious and hazardous individuals in every facet of your life.

WCIYB is an explanation, not an excuse, for people's inappropriate behavior. Color is a major stimulant in our lives and profoundly influences our behavior: the clothes we wear, the cars we drive, the advertisements that we read, or how we respond to the color of someone's hair, eyes, and skin. Historical, educational, religious, and/or cultural interpretations influence the environmental conditions that expose us to colors or the lack of colors. These influences may also have a subliminal effect on us.

The Yellow Brainers

The Yellow Brain section is the temporal lobe. There is a temporal lobe on both sides of the brain. Notice that the Yellow section contains a right angle. Yellow Brainers need to be "right." Rules are the foundation of a Yellow Brainer's life. They are recognized as left brain-critical thinkers who provide structure and stability in their professional and personal lives. Their punctuation mark is a period because they make declarations: "I'm the mom, that's why."

Historically, ancient Romans and Egyptians saw yellow as the color of their sun gods. Yellow can be mentally stimulating and boost your alertness. Many religions connect yellow to a spiritual path of unity, glory, and a supreme being or deity. Yellow also can represent power and wisdom. Yellow Brainers thrive on the responsibilities of leadership. They choose careers as CEOs, event planners, educators, bankers, business managers, and administrators and build their self-confidence with behavior that is "as good as gold." A traffic signal represents a Yellow Brainer's "I like to be in control" attitude.

The Blue Brainers

The Blue Brain circular section is the occipital lobe. It is located at the back of the brain and relates to the physical ability to see. It symbolizes insightfulness and the attribute to connect with others. Blue Brainers' intuition correlates with their creative-right side of the brain thinking and their "sky's the limit" perspective. Their punctuation mark is a question mark. They like to ask questions about other people to learn more about them. They often have to ask questions because they were talking and did not hear what was being said.

Historically, the Romans and Greeks attributed blue to Venus, the goddess of love. The Blue Brainers' perspective is one of love and peace. Blue has been used in studies to relax muscles, lower blood pressure, and was found to calm hyperactive children. In the Buddhist tradition, blue produces peace of mind and equanimity. Blue also represents the sky, coolness, and water. All three meanings symbolize a Blue Brainer's ability to be in the creative flow. The ancient Greeks said blue is the color of truth. Blue Brainers thrive on being "true blue." They choose careers as artists, social workers, musicians, childcare providers, and pet care specialists and build their self-confidence on truthfulness, authenticity, and helping others. A lightbulb represents a Blue Brainer's "I've got a great idea" attitude.

The Green Brainers

The Green Brain section, at the top of the brain, is the parietal lobe. It is a mini-computer that integrates information processing. Green Brainers are proficient problem solvers, avid readers, and adept with computers. They need to be independent and like to work by themselves. Their punctuation mark is a comma. Left-brain critical thinkers need to pause and contemplate what they are going to say before they speak. They never want to look or feel stupid.

Historically, green has symbolized growth, tranquility, and freshness. Green can reduce stress and be calming. In various cultures, green represents hope, long life, and immortality. The Hindu tradition states that green is the symbol of knowledge, memory, and the ability to see into the future. Green Brainers are visionaries who thrive on innovation and choose careers as accountants, computer professionals, scientific and medical researchers, engineers, and lawyers, and build their self-confidence by acquiring and imparting knowledge and solving problems. A "do not disturb" sign represents a Green Brainer's "I want to be alone to think" attitude.

The Orange Brainers

The Orange Brain asymmetrical section is the frontal lobe that takes the longest to mature. Its shape represents the Orange Brainers' fluid thoughts and actions. The Orange Brainers appear to be constantly on the move, physically and mentally. This movement represents their ability to create change and be thought of as right-brain creative thinkers. You have probably guessed the Orange Brain punctuation mark—an exclamation point, of course. They thrive on excitement, action, adventure, and risk-taking and build their self-confidence with their ability to get results.

Historically, according to Chinese tradition, orange represents a powerful energy source and stimulator. To the Japanese, it signifies happiness and love. Buddhist monks wear orange robes as a symbol of humility. Orange is a mixture of red and yellow that symbolizes excitement, energy, and the glowing flame of a fire. Orange is reported to boost the appetite and stimulate communication. Orange Brainers choose careers as firefighters, emergency room physicians and nurses, law enforcement officers, sports professionals, construction workers, and sales professionals. A juggler, keeping a variety of objects in the air, represents an Orange Brainer's "I can do it all" attitude.

It's Not Easy Being Green

When I am conducting a WCIYB workshop, I ask for a show of hands to demonstrate the Brain Color statistics of the American adult population.

- 35-40% Yellow Brain
- 35-40% Blue Brain
- 10-15% Green Brain
- 10-15% Orange Brain

Depending on the composition of the attendees, the numbers will vary. For example, a workshop for administrative assistants will have more Yellow Brainers, elementary school teachers more Blue Brainers, engineers more Green Brainers, and sales professionals more Orange Brainers.

The previous percentages demonstrate the diversity in a group, such as a chamber of commerce or community service organization. Unless the group is technology- or engineering-oriented, the smallest percentage of hands raised will invariably be the Green Brainers. They do not like to stand out in a crowd. Unlike the enthusiastic Orange Brainers, they hesitate, look around to see who else is Green, then reluctantly raise their hands. That is my cue to bring Jim Henson's celebrated Muppet, Kermit the Frog, stage center. Then I ask the group, "What does Kermit say?" and a chorus of "It's not easy being green!" echoes through the room.

It's not easy for the Green Brainers because they are the most misunderstood. They are not as comfortable demonstrating or communicating their feelings as the other Brain Colors. Actually, the Green Brainers can be more sensitive than the other Brain Colors, they just don't wear their hearts on their sleeves. Yellow Brainers say it's not easy for them because they worry about responsibilities; Blue Brainers because they become overwhelmed about personal issues; and Orange Brainers because their excitement creates too many activities for them to realistically handle.

"Only the Shadow Knows"

When any of the Brain Colors say "it's not easy," that indicates they are feeling what Carl Jung would describe as "Shadowed"—the subconscious negative or dark side of your personality. Historic and cultural symbols of the shadow include snakes (as in the Garden of Eden), dragons, monsters, demons, and the devil.

If your Comfort Color is "Shadowed" you may feel boxed in, restricted, stereotyped, labeled, or defined in a way that does not make you feel positive, confident, or trusting about yourself and others.

Notice that the head in the Brain Color logo seems to be pushing out of the box. WCIYB allows you to expand your personality and become more than you appear to be. Observe that the Brain Color head is not precise and the shadow of the head does not exactly fit the illustration. These imperfections are a visual metaphor of our personalities: No one likes to be put in a box or feel like they must be perfect.

A "Shadowed" Orange Brainer, who thrives on creative chaos, might find it difficult to understand and work with a Yellow Brainer who thinks the Orange Brainer is unreliable, because the Yellow Brainer values structure and accountability.

A "Shadowed" Green Brainer, who focuses on the problem, not the emotion that the problem creates, might find it difficult to understand and work with a Blue Brainer who feels hurt by what he or she feels is a Green Brainer's lack of sensitivity.

How Are You Feeling?

Understanding that individuals can be a silhouette of themselves will help you interpret "I'm not feeling like myself today" from a Brain Color perspective. You will learn more about your "Shadowed" personality and how it affects conflict and compatibility in Chapter 13: No-Brainer Conflict Resolution.

Understanding Your Color Combinations

Sir Isaac Newton discovered that when a prism broke up light, it revealed a continuous play of color—a rainbow. By definition, a rainbow is:

- a spectrum of brilliant color.
- highly varied or multifaceted.
- any multicolored arrangement or display.

Your Brainbow

The structure and relationship between the colors in a rainbow is not definitive. The colors harmoniously blend one into the next, just as you will learn to blend your Brain Colors to reduce conflict and increase harmony in your life.

You could select one or all of the definitions to describe your Brain Colors, or "Brainbow." In the previous chapters, you gained insight into each personality type's strengths and perspectives, and how you can appreciate their differences. Now that you have identified the numerical sequence of your Brain Colors, you can examine the full range of your Brainbow to appreciate the contrasting and complementary Brain Colors.

The four Brain Color designators are:

- Comfort Color.
- Blending Color.
- Convertible Color.
- Clouded Color.

The color you determined to have the highest value on your Brain Color Quiz is your **Comfort Color**. The highest possible value for any Brain Color is 48. It is your dominant Brain Color. It represents your strengths and comfort level in most situations. One of my clients discovered that her Comfort Color is Blue. Her B TOTAL of 43 out of a possible 48 demonstrates that she glows like a neon blue lightbulb! She sees herself as creative and flexible, and feels the most comfortable in communicative and cooperative situations.

The color you determined to be the second highest value is your **Blending Color**. Depending on its numerical ranking, it influences your Comfort Color and helps you easily shift between those two Brain Colors. The D TOTAL of 34 is my client's Orange Blending Color, an indication of her courageous and enthusiastic attitude, which influences her entrepreneurship.

The color you determined to be third in value is your **Convertible Color**. It is in the median ranking and can exchange positions with your Blending Color or Clouded Color. My client's A total of 26 is her Yellow Convertible Color. She often feels like the woman in her painting, *The Responsible Woman*, flying through the air carrying symbols of her home, career, family, friends, and community. The 34 Orange of her Blending Color and 26 Yellow of her Convertible Color demonstrate that she can easily switch back and forth between those two colors to become a resourceful woman.

The color you determined to have the lowest rank is your **Clouded Color**. It often is the spark that ignites conflict with yourself and others. The Clouded Color designator of my client's personality is her lowest ranking of 17 in the C (Green) TOTAL. She is diligent about using her Green brain instead of her Blue heart. When people make a request of her she says, "I need to time to think about that" before she offers an answer or makes a commitment. She also has learned to be grateful for the Green Brainers in her life. They compensate for her analytical deficiencies and encourage her when her personality is "Shadowed."

You can learn more about the concept of Shadowed in Chapter 3: Appreciate Our Differences and Chapter 13: No-Brainer Conflict Resolution.

Making Harmony Happen

The awareness of your Brain Color combinations will help you avoid conflicts and create more harmony in your life with yourself and others.

Specific colors blend while others conflict. As you learn more about your Brain Colors, it will become obvious that the Yellow perspective will have more difficulty blending with Orange, as will Green with Blue. Conversely, the Blue perspective will blend easily with the Orange and the Yellow with the Green.

If the numerical sequence of your Brain Colors is equally distributed and numerically balanced, you will find it easier to blend your Brain Colors. You also will be more adaptable, accepting, and patient with others and yourself. Conversely, if the numerical sequence is unequally distributed and numerically imbalanced you will find the opposite to be true.

"I'm Off the Chart!"

An example of this imbalance was in a **WCIYB** workshop I facilitated for the staff of a large community association. The organization was plagued with conflict between the domineering executive director and the staff, board of directors, and members at large. After the group completed their Brain Color Quizzes and placed corresponding colored dots on their nametags in the numerical sequence of their Brain Colors, laughter and banter permeated the room.

The executive director looked like a drum majorette as she marched up to the podium, plucked the microphone from my hand and announced, "I'm off the chart yellow! I'm 48-Yellow, 36-Green, 24-Blue, and 12-Orange." Her authoritarian and inflexible behavior now made perfect sense to everyone.

The "executive dictator" never became a Mother Theresa clone. However, with her new awareness of her Brain Colors and support from her staff, she became an adaptable administrator and delicate delegator, which contributed to the success of her organization.

A Comfortable Blending

Your Comfort Color and your Blending Color are your first and second colors; they have the most influence on your perspective and behavior. Consequently, if your Comfort Color is Yellow and your Blending Color is Orange, you are a "Yellow/Orange Brainer." Use this model whenever you blend two Brain Colors. The more your Comfort Color score exceeds your Blending Color score, the more dominant your Comfort Color will be.

Your Comfort Color/Blending Color combination can be complementary or conflicting. As you may have noticed, the Yellow and Orange characteristics are usually opposite each other; likewise, the Blue is opposite Green. As a result, Yellow/Orange Brainers experience conflict because their Yellow sense of responsibility clashes with their Orange desire for fun; the Blue/Green Brainers struggle between their Blue emotions and their Green logic.

Your Brain Colors or combinations can influence and benefit other people's Brain Colors, as theirs can influence and benefit yours. A Yellow Brainer can influence a Blue Brainer's decision about his garden. The benefit: the flowers and plants thrive because they are growing in the right soil, light, and water conditions. An Orange Brainer can influence a Green Brainer's indecision about remodeling her office. The benefit: recommendations for quality furniture and functional storage units that can be purchased at reasonable prices and installed by a reliable contractor.

Know Your Strengths

During a conference workshop for outdoor education instructors, attendees learned about their Brain Colors before they participated in team-building activities. I encouraged them to be aware of, appreciate, and apply their Brain Color knowledge during the activities. It was fascinating to observe the interaction between the participants, who had not known each other before the conference.

- The Yellow Brainers: explained the rules and organized the group into smaller teams.
- The Blue Brainers: encouraged each participant as they navigated the course, and congratulated them when they finished.

- The Green Brainers: evaluated the obstacle risks and developed systems everyone could utilize to complete the course safely.
- The Orange Brainers: eagerly demonstrated techniques to nimbly walk the tightrope, quickly negotiate obstacles, and cooperatively pass teammates through a giant rope web.

Knowing the strengths of their Comfort and Blending Colors positively influenced their diverse attributes and abilities, enhanced their self-confidence, and motivated them to work as a team to complete the obstacle course successfully.

Brainbow Combinations

The following examples of possible **Comfort**, **Blending**, and/or **Convertible** colors will help you recognize and value the following Brainbow combinations:

YELLOW BRAINBOW COMBINATIONS

- Yellow/Yellow: Dependable/Planner
- Yellow/Blue Brainer: Responsible/Nurturer
- Yellow/Green Brainer: Prepared/Researcher
- Yellow/Orange Brainer: Organized/Negotiator

BLUE BRAINBOW COMBINATIONS

- Blue/Blue: Sensitive/Naturalist
- Blue/Orange Brainer: Creative/Improviser
- Blue/Yellow Brainer: Affectionate/Caretaker
- Blue/Green Brainer: Helpful/Innovator

GREEN BRAINBOW COMBINATIONS

- Green/Green: Curious/Inventor
- Green/Yellow Brainer: Well informed/Planner
- Green/Blue Brainer: Technical/Trainer
- Green/Orange Brainer: Independent/Sales professional

ORANGE BRAINBOW COMBINATIONS

- Orange/Orange: Resourceful/Negotiator
- Orange/Blue Brainer: Risk-taker/Team player
- Orange/Yellow Brainer: Fun-loving/Organizer
- Orange/Green Brainer: Entrepreneurial/Problem solver

Your Reality

The combinations of your Brainbow are significant because your contrasting and complementary Brain Colors can vibrate to create tension, as well as talent. Your Brainbow perspective is your reality!

HOW OTHER COLORS SEE YOU

"For what you see and hear depends a good deal on where you are standing; it also depends on what kind of person you are."
—C.S. Lewis

Brain Color Glasses

How we see another person is similar to a writer's point of view (POV), which is the perspective of the story or character and how that viewpoint is revealed. To reveal your POV, imagine wearing a pair of Brain Color glasses that are tinted Yellow, Blue, Green, or Orange. However, how you see yourself may not be how others see you because of their Brain Color glasses. In specific situations, their POV might be more significant than how you see yourself.

Black Leather

During my workshops, I reinforce this concept by asking participants to collaborate with another person and share something about themselves that their partner would not know from their appearance or by speaking to them. This is the "true confessions" entertainment segment of the workshop. People have discovered that their receptionist is a champion horsewoman and their accountant is an accomplished fly-fisherman.

To the attendees, my physical appearance and conduct conveys that I am a capable and responsible businesswoman. Then, when it is my turn, I don my black hat with orange flames and a Harley Davidson logo and confess, "What you cannot tell by looking at me is… I am a 'Harley Mama' and ride on the back of a 'Bagger' in black leather." As a "biker babe," I make my point.

Depending on other people's Brain Color perspectives, you might be surprised to see how they see you and understand their positive or negative perception. This was true when my husband and I were on one of our annual motorcycle vacations. We were out riding one morning and decided to stop in a jewelry and gift store that friends told us not to miss. Dressed in our leathers, it was fascinating to observe how deliberately the salespeople ignored us. I decided to conduct a Brain Color experiment, so later that day we returned to the same store dressed in our conventional tourist clothes.

Several of the same salespeople approached us to ask if we needed any help. "No thank you," I said. "We are just looking." However, we were not looking at the merchandise, we were looking at them. They needed the help. Their perception of how a buyer should look cost them a possible sale and customer satisfaction.

The charts starting on page 32 will show you how others positively and negatively see your Brain Colors according to their POV.

"Sweetest"

It is easy to recognize your own admirable personality traits and difficult and uncomfortable to recognize the annoying ones. However, if you utilize the **WCIYB** approach, I think you will be more comfortable with yourself and accepting of others.

One morning, the meeting planner for a health care providers' association introduced to me to the workshop participants. The Orange/Blue Brainer concluded the introduction with: "and Sheila is one of the sweetest people I know!"

I responded to the "sweetest" comment with a grimace that made everyone laugh. As I stepped to the podium, I added, "Your colleague and I did not plan this, but this is a perfect example of why you are here this morning. She sees me as sweet, but I would never describe myself as sweet…kind or caring, but *not* sweet!"

The meeting planner used her Orange/Blue brain to be spontaneous and helpful about introducing me. Because I am Blue/Orange, I was not offended. I knew she was being creative with my introduction. In fact,

I was delighted that she contributed her personal feelings to the group, because it gave me the opportunity to comment on how her behavior transferred and applied to the program.

If Ms. Orange were Yellow or Green, she would not have ad libbed. She would have respected my request and read the introduction as I asked. We could not have created a better introduction or interaction with the group if we had planned it.

POV

Fundamentally, we differ in our values, needs, motivations, wants, and beliefs. **WCIYB** will help you understand that you cannot change another person. You can only change your POV about them through recognition and appreciation for their strengths and perspective. However, it is easier to see your POV, and someone else's, when you are wearing Brain Color glasses.

Author David Kiersey wrote, "If I do not want what you want, please do not try to tell me that my want is wrong. Or if I believe other than you, at least pause before you correct my view."

HOW OTHERS SEE YOUR BRAIN COLORS—THE YELLOW BRAINER PERSPECTIVE

Yellow sees Yellow:	Yellow sees Green:	Yellow sees Blue:	Yellow sees Orange:
Organized	Abstract	Honest	Impulsive
Dependable	To the point	Harmonious	Impatient
Conservative	Problem solver	Spiritual	Fun
Loyal	Smart	Genuine	Opportunistic
Predictable	Perfectionist	Devoted	Manipulative
Tenacious	Reserved	Sensitive	Out of control
Traditional	Boring	Compassionate	Manic
Stable	Logical	Sympathetic	Impulsive
Decisive	Smart	Helpful	Creative
Punctual	Independent	Emotional	Disorganized
Responsible	Superior	Compassionate	Late
Realistic	Withdrawn	Intuitive	Messy
Firm	Non-social	Indecisive	Belligerent
Effective	Condescending	Team players	Active
Caretaker	Thinkers, not Doers	Moody	Impractical

continued

HOW OTHERS SEE YOUR BRAIN COLORS—THE BLUE BRAINER PERSPECTIVE

Blue sees Blue:	Blue sees Yellow:	Blue sees Green:	Blue sees Orange:
Creative	Organized	Way too intelligent	Fly by seat of pants
Emotional	Anal retentive	Intimidating	Courageous
Intuitive	Not creative	Academic	Good sense of humor
Nurturing	Structured	No common sense	Disorganized
Communicative	Fighters for their point	No people skills	Not detail-oriented
Helpful	Not liking disruption	Too analytical	Just wants results
Moody	Rigid	Evaluating everything	Fun
Spiritual	Respectful	Inflexible	Annoying
Compassionate	Uncompromising	Smart	Adventurous
Pleaser	Self-righteous	Intense	Multi-task-oriented
Sympathetic	Goal-oriented	Focused	Carefree
Empathetic	Loyal	Cold	Adaptable
Harmonious	Neatniks	Uncaring	Enthusiastic
Trusting	Orderly	Independent	Competitive
Flexible	Executive type	Isolated	Expedient
Romantic	Domineering	Uncommunicative	Resourceful

continued

From *What Color Is Your Brain?* published by SLACK Incorporated. Copyright Sheila Glazov. www.whatcolorisyourbrain.com

HOW OTHERS SEE YOUR BRAIN COLORS—THE GREEN BRAINER PERSPECTIVE

Green sees Green:	Green sees Yellow:	Green sees Blue:	Green sees Orange:
Productive	Bureaucratic	Emotional	Impulsive
Logical	Controlling	Caring	Courageous
Innovative	Orderly	Empathetic	Cavalier
Knowledgeable	Organized	Relationship-focused	Spontaneous
Superior intellect	Task-oriented	Concerned	Intuitive
Curious	Computational	Warm	Fun
Fair-minded	Rigid	Smothering	Unreliable
Objective	Organized	Mothering	Illogical
Selective	Dependable	Valuable	Valueless
Precise	Traditional	Helpful	Spontaneous
Visionary	"Know-it-alls"	Too talkative	Inconsistent
Rational	Self-righteous	Idealistic	Self-absorbed
Reasonable	Historians	Touchy-feely	Change agent
Cool, calm, & collected	Planners	Fighters for a cause	Idea generator
Efficient	Prompt	Creative	Impetuous

continued

From *What Color Is Your Brain?* published by SLACK Incorporated. Copyright Sheila Glazov. www.whatcolorisyourbrain.com

HOW OTHERS SEE YOUR BRAIN COLORS—THE ORANGE BRAINER PERSPECTIVE

Orange sees Orange:	*Orange sees Yellow:*	*Orange sees Blue:*	*Orange sees Green:*
Decisive	Controlling	Friendly	Nerds
Capable	Organized	Sensitive	Fact finders
Smart	Scheduling	Romantic	Eggheads
Fast moving	Structured	Creative	Geeks
Influential	Opinionated	Poetic	Number crunchers
Not liking routine	Stubborn	Caring	Studious
Fun-loving	Inflexible	Lovers	Slow moving
Hands-on learner	Jailers	Helpful	Analyzers
Skillful	Self-righteous	Cooperative	Plodding
Good negotiator	Frustrating	Loving	Intellectual
Problem solver	Judgmental	Understating	Dull
Proficient	Too scared	Compassionate	Dry
Athletic	Boring	Listeners	Insensitive
Results provider	Stringent	Nurturers	Ice cold
Risk taker	Safe	Intuitive	Condescending

From *What Color Is Your Brain?* published by SLACK Incorporated. Copyright Sheila Glazov. www.whatcolorisyourbrain.com

A Different POV

I encourage you to pause before you tell someone he or she is wrong or attempt to correct his or her POV, and consider the POV that Glenn Frank, American editor and educator, offers in his poem, *The Difference.*

When the other fellow acts that way,
He is ugly;
When you do, it's nerves.

When the other fellow is set in his ways,
He is obstinate;
When you do, it's firmness.

When the other fellow takes his time,
He is dead slow;
When you do, you are deliberate.

When the other fellow treats someone especially well,
He is toadying;
When you do, it's tact.

When the other fellow finds fault,
He's cranky;
When you do, you are discriminating.

When the other fellow says what he thinks,
He is spiteful;
When you do, you are frank.

THRIVE IN IDEAL CONDITIONS

Ideal conditions provide an opportunity for each Brain Color to thrive. Providing a climate where individuals feel safe and free to explore their own ideas and feelings develops their creative problem-solving techniques, improves their decision-making skills, and enhances their self-esteem.

Morale Problems

An urgent phone call from one of my clients, who is Vice President of a bank and a Yellow Brainer, validated this finding. "Our department is developing morale problems due to the establishment of a new computer system. We're having continuous employee turnover," she said. "The Blue Brainers are not comfortable or confident about learning a new computer program and the Yellow Brainers are upset about the disorganization and staff instability."

We immediately scheduled a workshop. During the program, the Yellow Brainers recognized their discomfort and learned new skills that would help them adapt to the personnel changes. The Blue Brainers identified their discomfort, learned how they could adjust to the technological changes, and became excited about the new computer skills. Her department staff re-established their ideal working conditions within a month.

Educational, economic, or cultural influences can negatively or positively affect the ideal conditions in your home, workplace, school, or community.

Ideal Conditions at Home

YELLOW BRAINERS

- An orderly atmosphere
- Rules or guidelines
- Personal safety
- Financial security
- Structured routines

BLUE BRAINERS

- Creative expression
- Interaction and communication
- Harmony
- Family and social activities
- Cooperation

GREEN BRAINERS

- Privacy
- Defined expectations
- Acknowledgment for expertise and skills
- State-of-the-art equipment
- Quiet alone time

ORANGE BRAINERS

- Recognition of their need for freedom
- An outlet for their energetic style
- Appreciation for taking action when needed
- Understanding for getting tasks done in their own time frame
- Opportunities for having FUN

Ideal Conditions at Work

YELLOW BRAINERS

- Long-term company planning
- Recognition for a job well done
- Company manuals and procedures
- Well-trained support staff
- Definitive job description and responsibilities

BLUE BRAINERS

- Interaction between employees
- Shared decision making
- Relaxed company policies
- Flexible work schedule
- Personalized work space

GREEN BRAINERS

- State-of-the-art equipment
- Research resources
- Independent work schedules
- Opportunities to use problem-solving skills
- Innovative systems

ORANGE BRAINERS

- Immediate monetary rewards for achieving results
- A variety of challenges
- Locations for relaxation and/or physical recreation
- No schedules or meetings
- Freedom to take action

Is It Nature or Nurture?

By now, you might be wondering how nature and nurture affect an individual's personality. Is your personality determined by your environment or gene pool? My fundamental nature vs. nurture belief is this: the conditions of an environment or setting have a significant effect on the nurturing of an individual's natural temperament. I agree with the premise that an individual's personality is a combination of both the person's natural characteristics (nature) and how he or she is raised (nurture), which determine personality traits and behavior.

We are living in a time of rapid change, which significantly impacts your Brain Colors. Sometimes the conditions of your surroundings or another person's behavior can cause you to feel uncomfortable or unsafe.

A specific environment will nurture the natural traits of an individual. A Green Brainer and a Yellow Brainer will not be as comfortable or productive in an unscheduled brainstorming session as a Blue Brainer or an Orange Brainer.

Opposite Brain Color settings, as long as the environment is trustworthy, can nurture your natural attributes and abilities. Trustworthiness is the ability to accept others and their contributions, to support, recognize, and affirm others' strengths and capabilities, and exhibit cooperative and honest intention. People thrive when their attributes and abilities are acknowledged!

You are capable of changing your environment and making conscious decisions to nurture yourself. Some Brain Colors adapt to change easier than others do. You will learn more about what prompts you to change in Chapter 14: You Can Change Your Brain Color.

To enhance your awareness of the ideal conditions in which your Brain Color thrives, you need to be alert. If you are watchful, you will recognize the characteristics that reveal an individual's Brain Color.

Yellow Brainer = Clean-Up Coaches

- *Office*: Their workspace and desk are clear of any clutter. Awards are hung sequentially and straight on the wall. It is so neat it looks as if no one works there.

- *Home*: Their living space resembles a homebuilder's model house. Each room has an abundance of storage space that is organized like a department store showcase. Yellow Brainers do not keep what they do not use. Be careful, don't stand still, you might be thrown out, given to a charity, or tagged for the garage sale!

Blue Brainer = Cozy Collectors

- *Office*: Their work space looks like someone's family room. It is accessorized with comfortable furnishings, flowers, memorabilia, and family or pet photos.
- *Home*: Their living space has a welcoming and "lived in" feeling. Absolutely no 1950s plastic furniture covers for the Blue Brainers. Family pictures decorate the walls and tabletops. They collect loving keepsakes.

Green Brainer = Selective Savers

- *Office*: The desk is large enough to keep all their projects within reaching distance. They will have the latest technology, a collection of books on the floor or shelves, and their diplomas displayed on the wall.
- *Home*: Their living space also has the latest technology and/or piles of newspapers or magazines. They keep everything that might contain information, because "someday that information could be important." A private area or getaway to enjoy some peace and quiet is a requirement.

Orange Brainer = Clutter Champions

- *Office*: Their desk is anything that works, because they do not spend a lot of time there. Organizing their office is a waste of time and the floor looks like a display of stalagmites. If you comment about their décor, they will profess, "I know exactly what's in each pile." However, you might need a GPS to navigate their workspace if they ask you to find something they need when they are outside of the office.

- *Home*: Their living area is usually cluttered. Photos of their adventures adorn the walls. Of course, they would rather have fun than clean up. All kinds of sports or hobby paraphernalia are stored in the garage or basement for easy access.

Alert!

Remain alert to the ideal conditions in which your Brain Colors will thrive. Your awareness is essential for building your confidence, solving problems, and making healthy decisions in your workplace, home, or community.

SECTION I: BRAIN COLOR CONNECTIONS SUMMARY

Brain Color	Yellow Brainers	Blue Brainers	Green Brainers	Orange Brainers
Perspective	Dependable	Helpful	Logical	Dynamic
Strengths	Responsible, Loyal, Prepared, Practical, Punctual	Flexible, Creative, Cooperative, Kind, Compassionate	Knowledgeable, Competent, Calm, Technical, Curious	Generous, Fun, Resourceful, Eager, Energetic
Brain Lobes	Temporal	Occipital	Parietal	Frontal
"Shadowed" Behavior	Anxious & Worried	Depressed & Passive Resistant	Withdrawn & Indecisive	Rude & "Dropping out"
Ideal Home Conditions	Orderly & Financially Secure	Harmonious & Communicative	Private & Quiet	Unstructured & Active
Ideal Workplace Conditions	Procedures & Trained Staff	Relaxed policies & Personalized space	Independence & Innovative systems	Challenges & No meetings
How Other People See Them	Realistic, Orderly, Controlling, Rigid, Accountable	Nurturing, Caring, Moody, Smothering, Trustworthy	Visionary, Efficient, Insensitive, Intense, Intelligent	Skillful, Decisive, Unreliable, Unstable, Adventurous

From *What Color Is Your Brain?* published by SLACK Incorporated. Copyright Sheila Glazov. www.whatcolorisyourbrain.com

SECTION II

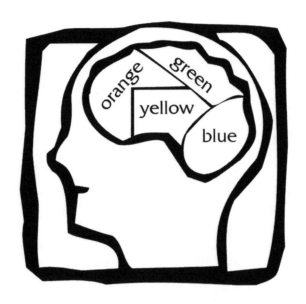

PERSONAL BRAIN COLOR
CONNECTIONS

YOUR ROMANTIC RELATIONSHIPS

"It's relationships that spark me."
—Stephen Sondheim, composer and lyricist

Beware!

The spark that ignites your positive attraction can fizzle into a negative reaction. Your "soul mate" may become a "cell mate" and your "dearest friend" a "dreadful fiend."

Today, scientists, doctors, psychologists, and sociologists believe that men's and women's brains are wired differently. According to Anne Moir, Ph.D., co-author of *Brain Sex*, "The sexes are different because their brains are different. The brain, the chief administrative and emotional organ of life, is differently constructed in men and in women; it processes information in a different way, which results in different perceptions, priorities, and behaviour."

I Got It!

After presenting WCIYB to an Adult Learning Theory class, I enjoyed several informal discussions with the students. However, there was one conversation that I was honored to share and still resonates with me. A delightful gentleman with a sparkle of recognition in his eyes shook my hand with both of his and said, "Thank you. I've been married for 30 years and now I *finally* understand my wife. I'm green and she is blue!"

Contrast and Complement

In personal relationships, contrasting colors can complement or destroy a romantic relationship. My theory is supported by the research of J. Philippe Rushton, Ph.D., D.Sc., Professor of Psychology at the University of Western Ontario in Canada, and Dr. Neil Clark Warren, clinical psychologist and founder of eHarmony. Dr. Rushton states, "Happiness and stability can be predicted by matching of personal attributes." In his book, *Date or Soul Mate? How to Know if Someone Is Worth Pursuing in Two Dates or Less*, Dr. Warren states, "You can expect to attract a person whose total set of attributes is approximately equal to your own."

Learn to Share

Each Brain Color has opportunities to share their attributes and abilities to enrich their romantic relationships.

- The Yellow Brainer gives guidelines and is a financial planner.
- The Blue Brainer gives cooperation and is a social worker.
- The Green Brainer gives knowledge and is a technical consultant.
- The Orange Brainer gives energy and is a resourceful troubleshooter.

I believe an enduring romantic relationship develops if a couple appreciates their contrasting and complementary Brain Colors and respects what the other individual values. The chart starting on page 52 will help you appreciate each Brain Color's perspective in a romantic relationship.

What Attracts You?

In a romantic relationship, a variety of personal characteristics and talents attracts us to another individual.

A Blue Brainer once confided in me that she was attracted to a Green Brainer. However, she could not figure out the attraction until I said, "You're attracted to him because he is a fire fighter."

"No he's not, he's a systems analyst."

"Exactly! He's always putting out fires," I replied.

"I got it! But, if he's not available or interested in me, I'll really be blue," she laughed.

YELLOW BRAINERS ARE ATTRACTED TO:

- Yellow Brainers who respect their rules.
- Orange Brainers who contribute adventure to their routine.
- Blue Brainers who cooperate on their projects.
- Green Brainers who provide structured systems for them.

BLUE BRAINERS ARE ATTRACTED TO:

- Blue Brainers who reciprocate their show of affection.
- Yellow Brainers who respect their feelings.
- Green Brainers who give them a logical perspective.
- Orange Brainers who encourage their creativity.

GREEN BRAINERS ARE ATTRACTED TO:

- Green Brainers who also value solitude.
- Blue Brainers who are thoughtful.
- Yellow Brainers who keep precise records.
- Orange Brainers who seize opportunities.

ORANGE BRAINERS ARE ATTRACTED TO:

- Orange Brainers who will join in their fun.
- Blue Brainers who encourage their enthusiasm.
- Green Brainers who help them calculate risk.
- Yellow Brainers who plan their activities.

Mess-Ups

The following quotes demonstrate how you can make a mess of a model romance:

continued on page 54

MY YELLOW ROMANTIC BRAIN PERSPECTIVE

I VALUE: Commitment
I AM NATURALLY: Loyal and practical
MY PERSONAL ATTITUDE IS: Serious
EMOTIONALLY I NEED TO: Be in control
I LIKE DATES THAT ARE: Planned
MY FINANCIAL APPROACH IS: Money in the bank
MY SOCIAL ATTITUDE IS: "It's on my calendar."
MY COMMUNICATION STYLE IS: Direct and directive
MY PRIORITY IS: Plans for the future
MY STRESS FACTOR IS: Plans not being valued
I'M PHYSICALLY ATTENTIVE: At appropriate times
MY RELIGIOUS OBSERVANCE IS: Conventional
I LIKE GREETING CARDS THAT ARE: Sentimental

 MY BLUE ROMANTIC BRAIN PERSPECTIVE

I VALUE: Compassion
I AM NATURALLY: Affectionate and peaceful
MY PERSONAL ATTITUDE IS: Enthusiastic
EMOTIONALLY I NEED TO: Feel appreciated
I LIKE DATES THAT ARE: Romantic
MY FINANCIAL APPROACH IS: Money isn't a priority
MY SOCIAL ATTITUDE: "Invite the whole neighborhood!"
MY COMMUNICATION STYLE IS: Anything on my mind
MY PRIORITY: Peace and harmony
MY STRESS FACTOR: My feelings are not being validated
I'M PHYSICALLY ATTENTIVE: As much as possible
MY RELIGIOUS OBSERVANCE IS: Spiritual
I LIKE GREETING CARDS THAT ARE: Mushy

MY GREEN ROMANTIC BRAIN PERSPECTIVE

I VALUE: Calmness

I AM NATURALLY: Reserved and private

MY PERSONAL ATTITUDE IS: Purposeful

I EMOTIONALLY NEED TO: Be selective

I LIKE DATES THAT ARE: Secluded

MY FINANCIAL APPROACH IS: An accounting system

MY SOCIAL ATTITUDE: "Do I have to go?"

MY COMMUNICATION STYLE: Only when necessary

MY PRIORITY IS: No drama

MY STRESS FACTOR IS: Not enough time to myself

I AM PHYSICALLY ATTENTIVE: When no one's watching

MY RELIGIOUS OBSERVANCE IS: Scholarly

I LIKE GREETING CARDS THAT ARE: No-frills

MY ORANGE ROMANTIC BRAIN PERSPECTIVE

I VALUE: Adventure

I AM NATURALLY: Spontaneous and playful

MY PERSONAL ATTITUDE IS: Energizing

I EMOTIONALLY NEED TO: Feel uninhibited

I LIKE DATES THAT ARE: Active

MY FINANCIAL APPROACH IS: "When I've got it, I spend it!"

MY SOCIAL ATTITUDE IS: "Where's the party?"

MY COMMUNICATION STYLE IS: Expressive

MY PRIORITY IS: A good time

MY STRESS FACTOR IS: Others' plans interfere with mine

I AM PHYSICALLY ATTENTIVE: Anywhere, any time

MY RELIGIOUS OBSERVANCE IS: Non-traditional

I LIKE GREETING CARDS THAT ARE: Humorous

continued from page 51

- A Yellow Brainer asks a Green Brainer, "Did anyone in our family pass away today that you haven't told me about?"
- The Blue Brainer stops talking when the Green Brainer replies, "You don't have to repeat yourself. I heard you the first time."
- A Green Brainer hugs the Blue Brainer and whispers, "I save all my Blue for you, because you are my favorite person and I don't *have* to talk to you."
- An Orange Brainer says, "I want to go somewhere fun for our honeymoon." The Green Brainer responds, "Why?"

Do I Annoy You?

Often, we are drawn to another individual because they have personality traits and talents that we do not have or that we would like to have. Remember, what first attracted you in your romantic relationship might later annoy you.

YELLOW BRAINERS BECOME ANNOYED WHEN:

- Yellow Brainers crave more control.
- Blue Brainers act like scatter-brains.
- Green Brainers do not give them all the details.
- Orange Brainers do not respect their rules.

BLUE BRAINERS BECOME ANNOYED WHEN:

- Yellow Brainers restrain their creativity.
- Blue Brainers drain them with their extra drama.
- Green Brainers dismiss their feelings.
- Orange Brainers exhaust their enthusiasm.

GREEN BRAINERS BECOME ANNOYED WHEN:

- Yellow Brainers intrude on their solitude.
- Blue Brainers talk too much.
- Green Brainers insinuate that they know more.
- Orange Brainers "fire" before they "ready and aim."

ORANGE BRAINERS BECOME ANNOYED WHEN:

- Yellow Brainers restrict their fun.
- Blue Brainers coddle them.
- Green Brainers criticize them.
- Orange Brainers change their minds too often.

Love and Money

How individuals handle financial issues is often the number one reason for the success or failure of a romantic relationship. On a daily basis, the requirements of food, housing, and clothing can be disruptive. On, before, or after a life cycle event, such as a wedding or death of a family member, the purchase of a home or automobile, or paying for a college education, financial stresses can be catastrophic.

How each Brain Color manages their finances can determine compatibility or conflict. Olivia Mellan, author of *Money Harmony: Resolving Money Conflicts in Your Life and Your Relationships*, says, "Just as each person in a relationship has a different personality, they may also have different attitudes toward money…but if you talk about your differences, you may be able to work out a few compromises that keep the tension to a minimum."

Money Attitudes

In order to talk about your attitude toward money, you need to understand how your Brain Color influences your financial behavior.

Yellow Brainers consistently make deposits in a savings account and plan how much they are going to spend on their financial needs or desires. Orange Brainers think Yellow Brainers are nuts for not spending their money while they can enjoy it.

Blue Brainers do not give a second thought to their finances. People, not pennies, are more important to them. They will hire or ask a Green Brainer to help them with their finances. They do not think about how much they are spending, just how much they enjoy buying something for a friend or loved one.

Green Brainers enjoy spreadsheets and accounting for all their expenditures. They become frustrated with the Blue Brainers when they have to explain their accounting practices, what a budget is, and why they need one.

Orange Brainers are spenders, not savers, and their attitude drives Yellow Brainers crazy. The Yellow Brainers often irritate the Orange Brainers because they want to limit their spending and teach them how to be financially responsible.

Green Brainers and Yellow Brainers appreciate each other's financial attitude toward budgeting and saving money. Blue Brainers and Orange Brainers others understand each other's financial attitude toward enjoying and spending their money.

Balan¢e

Utilize your Brain Colors to balance your finances and your romantic relationships successfully.

YOUR RELATIONSHIPS
WITH CO-WORKERS

"We don't see things as they are. We see them as we are."
—Anaïs Nïn

The Little Canary

During a teambuilding workshop for a national real estate company, it was evident that the Orange Brain brokers agitated the Yellow Brain administrative assistants ("admins"). The admins' spokesperson said, "We're misunderstood and unappreciated. The brokers do *not* value timeliness, they mock our organizational requirements, and they are clueless about the admins' needs."

The brokers' spokesperson said, "We're concerned with getting the results we need, not the procedures that are connected to someone else's schedule."

After lunch, a Yellow Brain admin, who had been an English teacher in a previous career, read the following poem to the workshop participants.

We Yellow people are feeling very Blue,
Because of all the nasty things that were said about us.
We're Green with envy over all the positive attributes the rest of you seem to have.
Now, Orange you ashamed of yourselves for putting us down?
Signed,
Joan Fessler
Sweet, Nurturing, Intelligent, Fun-loving Little Canary

The Orange Brokers got the point and reciprocated. At the close of the workshop, an Orange Broker recited his poem:

The Orange Brainers need to have fun,
But without the Yellow Brainers nothing would get done!

It's easier to promote harmony and increase productivity when people's frustrations are recognized and they feel appreciated.

The chart on the facing page will help you understand your co-workers' frustrations and how you can build compatible and cooperative relationships in your workplace.

Work in Perfect Harmony

You will no longer have to think of your co-workers as prima donnas. Now that you know what frustrates them and makes them feel appreciated, you can become a barbershop quartet.

The meeting room at a social service agency reverberated with laughter when the staff members completed their Brain Color Quizzes. The noise level quickly elevated, while they stuck their Yellow, Blue, Green, and Orange dots on their nametags. Those moments of discovery are the prelude to a lively chorus of exclamations and harmonious banter.

"Oh, Michelle and I are exactly the same colors, no wonder we work so well together!"

"Now I know why I have such a hard time getting along and working with John; he's so Green and I'm so Blue!"

"I understand why my Orange needs Maureen's Yellow to get the job done!"

"It's incredible, that's why our team works in perfect harmony!"

It's a Puzzlement

"One of my most competent managers totally mystifies me," my client confided in me during a pre-workshop meeting. "I am at a loss for words to describe his baffling behavior. He's driving me crazy!"

"His staff is so frustrated and bewildered that every day one of them wants to quit. I hired him because he was referred to me with glowing professional references, but I didn't realize that his interpersonal skills

CO-WORKER BRAIN COLOR FRUSTRATIONS

Yellow Brain Frustrations

Not being in control

Disorder

Lack of preparation

Irresponsibility

Tardiness

Distractions

Poor or no directions/instructions

Blue Brain Frustrations

Apathy

Inconsideration

Lack of communication

Dishonesty

Insensitivity

Lack of cooperation

Conflict

Green Brain Frustrations

Intrusions

Not getting the big picture

Incomplete data

Lack of independent thinking

Redundancy

No forethought

Technical systems down

Orange Brain Frustrations

Someone else's schedule

Never enough time

Negativity

Lack of energy

Whining

Waiting

No action or results

were so inadequate." She continued, "How was I to know that he would behave like a raving tyrant when things just didn't go his way or one of his staff members would dare to give him a suggestion?"

"Sounds like you have a puzzle that is missing a few significant pieces," I suggested.

"Only a few?" she chuckled. "To look at him or see him in action with a client you would not believe we were talking about the same person. But how do I find the missing pieces to the puzzle?" "It's simple," I assured her. "The solution is understanding the manager's Brain Color and the staff members' perspective."

You may find your co-workers are like a puzzle. The following charts will help you recognize your boss', leader's, or manager's Brain Colors, and their characteristics according to your Brain Color perspective.

YELLOW BRAINER'S PERSPECTIVE OF BOSSES, LEADERS, AND/OR MANAGERS

Yellow Brainers See Yellow Brainers

Dependable

Effective

Practical

Impatient

Dedicated

Serious

Resistant to change

Yellow Brainers See Green Brainers

Brainy

Thorough

Focused

Insensitive

Secretive

Condescending

Yellow Brainers See Orange Brainers

Risk-takers

Self-starters

Clever

Immature

Uncooperative

Need for immediate gratification

Erratic

Yellow Brainers See Blue Brainers

Warm

Genuine

Sincere

Disorganized

Chatty

Ambiguous

continued

BLUE BRAINER'S PERSPECTIVE OF BOSSES, LEADERS, AND/OR MANAGERS

Blue Brainers See Blue Brainers

Compassionate
Good with feelings
Family focused
Too easygoing
Not focused
Emotional

Blue Brainers See Yellow Brainers

Structured
Perfectionists
List makers
Bossy
Demanding
Do it themselves

Blue Brainers See Orange Brainers

Spontaneous
Resourceful
Change agents
Procrastinators
Disorganized
Inconsiderate

Blue Brainers See Green Brainers

Intelligent
Independent
Logical
Unreasonable
Insensitive
Uncommunicative

continued

GREEN BRAINER'S PERSPECTIVE OF BOSSES, LEADERS, AND/OR MANAGERS

Green Brainers See Green Brainers

Systematic
Reasonable
Rational
Unemotional
Intense
Indecisive

Green Brainers See Blue Brainers

Forgiving
Harmonious
Innovative
Scattered
Illogical
Arbitrary

Green Brainers See Orange Brainers

Funny
Energetic
Ingenious
Disruptive
Unpredictable
Show-offs

Green Brainers See Yellow Brainers

Conventional
Reliable
Disciplinarians
Worriers
Fussy
Boring

continued

ORANGE BRAINER'S PERSPECTIVE OF BOSSES, LEADERS, AND/OR MANAGERS

Orange Brainers See Orange Brainers

Entertaining
Enthusiastic
Persuasive
Crazy
Exhausting
Unrealistic

Orange Brainers See Green Brainers

Smart
Technical
Instructive
Sticklers
Stand-offish
Snobbish

Orange Brainers See Yellow Brainers

Organized
Prompt
Practical
Bossy
Rigid
Completes task at expense of result

Orange Brainers See Blue Brainers

Nurturing
Trusting
Creative
Smothering
Hysterical
Conflicted

From *What Color Is Your Brain?* published by SLACK Incorporated. Copyright Sheila Glazov. www.whatcolorisyourbrain.com

The Solution

If you are unable to solve that which perplexes you, the solution becomes as complicated as a 1,000-piece picture puzzle. However, if you utilize the Brain Color Co-Workers perspectives chart, the puzzle becomes easy to solve.

To be productive and successful in the workplace, I encourage you to spend time discovering the puzzle pieces to your perspective, and understanding how to put them together and fit them into the appropriate places. If you do, you will decrease frustration, increase cooperation, and solve the puzzle with your co-workers!

YOUR RELATIONSHIPS WITH FAMILY MEMBERS AND FRIENDS

"The sharing of joy, whether physical, emotional, psychic, or intellectual, forms a bridge between the sharers which can be the basis for understanding much of what is not shared between them, and lessens the threat of their difference."
—Audre Lorde

Men, Women, and Brain Colors

By recognizing and appreciating the differences in your own Brain Colors, you can lessen the threat created by your differences with others and increase joy and understanding in your relationships, especially between men and women. According to Dr. Louann Brizendine in her book, *The Female Brain,* "Men and women have different brain sensitivities to stress and conflict. They use different areas and circuits to solve problems, process language, experience and store the same strong emotion. Women may remember the smallest details of their first dates, and their biggest fights, while their husbands barely remember that these things happened."

People question me about which gender is which Brain Color. My cumulative personal and professional observations are: a substantial number of women are Yellow and Blue Brainers and a substantial number of men are Green and Orange Brainers. In Chapter 3: Appreciate Our Differences, a sampling of Brain Color career choices also support my observations.

My college roommate and I validate my findings. She is a Yellow Brainer and I am a Blue Brainer. We were both teachers and enjoy "Blue" time with each other and with our children and grandchildren. Her husband is a Green Brainer and mine is an Orange Brainer. Both men are attorneys who are avid "Orange" sports enthusiasts.

Before the four of us understood and utilized **WCIYB**, our contrasting Comfort and Blending Colors created some irritating situations. Our female Yellow and Blue Brains clashed with their male Green and Orange Brains over spending time together as couples or watching sporting events on TV. Because of WCIYB, we have learned to accommodate and appreciate each other's contrasting Brain Colors, which has strengthened our individual relationships and our friendship between the four of us for over 40 years.

Who Fills Your Honeycomb?

When I think about my relationships with family members and friends, I visualize my heart as a honeycomb, with a compartment for each individual. However, at times, it has felt like the cast members from a soap opera have filled those compartments instead of cover models of *Family Circle* magazine. Think about who fills your honeycomb.

The chart on pages 72-73 will help you understand which Brain Color perspective influences the family members and friends who fill the compartments of your honeycomb.

Let's Take a Vacation

Imagine taking a Brain Color vacation with the soap opera cast members or magazine models. It will be an unforgettable opportunity to examine your "color-filled" relationships.

Yellow Brainers arrange for well-planned vacations. If they do not want to hire a guide or participate in a tour, they will do their homework ahead of time, plan the entire trip, and become the tour guide. Their family vacations are scheduled each year at the same time and the same place, such as a summer cottage or resort. Suitcases are prepared in advance. They also enjoy all-inclusive destinations that have planned activities for the children, as well as for themselves. If it is a driving trip, they have checked with AAA and purchased every map they will need for route A and alternative route B. They know the location of, and have a schedule for, every rest, fuel, or food stop and point of interest.

Blue Brainers love reunions with family members, close friends, class-mates and neighbors, as well as nature trips. They enjoy helping everyone get all their belongings ready and packed for their time together. Vacations are opportunities to share time with everyone they love. Since their pets are part of the family, they take them along and stay in accommodations that are advertised as pet friendly. They enjoy a homey atmosphere where they can chat with the proprietor and other guests in small inns, bed & breakfasts, or campsites. On a driving trip, they like to stop along the way to spend time with friends or family members. They love scenic spots where they can capture their memories, which will be set to music on a DVD or made into a scrapbook when they return home.

Green Brainers prefer to travel on their own or with a small group of individuals who share the same interest in what they are going to experi-ence. They enjoy investigatory or educational tours of significant historic events, museums, and ruins of ancient civilizations or locations where they can acquire work-related information. If they are visiting a foreign country, they will learn to speak the language and study the guidebooks to become familiar with the culture and customs. They have a system for packing their suitcases and only pack the essentials. They like to stay in accommodations that can give them the privacy and/or the technology they require or desire. They do their research and impart detailed facts and figures to their traveling companions about points of interest on their journey, which they have located and downloaded into their navigational global positioning system (GPS).

The Orange Brainers love spontaneity and variety for their vacations. They find unfamiliar or exotic places and meeting new people exciting. Sporting trips such as helicopter skiing, crewing on a sailboat, whitewater rafting, or going on an African safari are at the top of their list. They find it advantageous to do Yellow Brain planning to have the right equipment and reservations for their activities at the destination, even if it means ignoring other people's plans. Shopping for and purchasing the sporting equipment is almost as much fun as the vacation. Their accommodations do not have to be fancy; however, if they have the means, they will spend the money for the best. A spur of the moment trip or short weekend get-away is the perfect escape from the boredom of their daily routine. They will get in the car and continue driving until they find a place that looks interesting or entertaining. Rest and relaxation are a significant part of their vocabulary and a requirement to recover from their frantic fun.

YELLOW BRAIN FAMILY MEMBER AND FRIEND PERSPECTIVE

MY ATTITUDE IS: "Do it the *right* way, my way."

MY PERSONAL STYLE IS: Disciplined & dedicated

MY HOME IS: Orderly

WITH OTHERS: I inform them of "my" rules

I NEED: Schedules

MY FINANCIAL NEED: A savings account

I ENCOURAGE: Respectfulness & punctuality

I SHOW LOVE BY: Taking care of my family

I SOLVE PROBLEMS: By following procedures

MY STRESS FACTOR IS: Disrespectfulness & irresponsibility

WHEN I'M UPSET: I worry and give guilt trips

I RELAX: Only if everything is finished

BLUE BRAIN FAMILY MEMBER AND FRIEND PERSPECTIVE

MY ATTITUDE: "I'm behind you all the way."

MY PERSONAL STYLE IS: Thoughtful & devoted

MY HOME IS: Cozy

WITH OTHERS: I am an earnest listener & communicator

I NEED: Conversation

MY FINANCIAL NEED: None, I'm not concerned about money

I ENCOURAGE: Flexibility & enjoyment of nature

I SHOW LOVE WITH: Special gifts, hugs & kisses

I SOLVE PROBLEMS: By talking it over with others

MY STRESS FACTOR Overextending myself for others

WHEN I'M UPSET: I say "I'm fine," but I'm not

I RELAX: With friends, family, and pets

GREEN BRAIN FAMILY MEMBER AND FRIEND PERSPECTIVE

MY ATTITUDE IS: "Figure it out for yourself."

MY PERSONAL STYLE IS: I don't interfere & I'm objective

MY HOME IS: Quiet

WITH OTHERS: I'm not overly complimentary

I NEED: Efficiency

MY FINANCIAL NEED: Studying the risks & rewards

I ENCOURAGE: Self-sufficiency

I SHOWS LOVE WITH: Actions, not words

I SOLVE PROBLEMS: Unemotionally, with thorough thinking

MY STRESS FACTOR: Others meddling in my business

WHEN I'M UPSET: I give off the "Big Chill"

I RELAX: By myself

ORANGE BRAIN FAMILY MEMBER AND FRIEND PERSPECTIVE

MY ATTITUDE IS: "Give it your best shot."

MY PERSONAL STYLE IS: Fraternal & optimistic

MY HOME IS: Cluttered

WITH OTHERS: I let them be themselves

I NEED: Variety

MY FINANCIAL NEED: Have fun spending money

I ENCOURAGE: Taking risks

I SHOW LOVE WITH: Surprises and gifts

I SOLVE PROBLEMS: In the moment with quick reactions

MY STRESS FACTOR: Others telling me what to do

WHEN I'M UPSET: I say, "I'm out of here!"

I RELAX: With physical activity

Say It in Color

Whether you are at home or on a vacation, the following tips can help enhance your relationships with family members and friends.

- When asking someone to finish their chores around the house, to be on time for an event, or pack their suitcase for a trip, say, "I'd like you to be Yellow..."

- If you need someone to give you a hand with the dinner dishes, put his or her wet swimsuit on the line at the summer cabin, or help an elderly relative get seated for a picture at a reunion, say, "I need you to be Blue..."

- If you are having a problem getting your children to do their homework, you don't want to waste time or get lost on a road trip, or you can't figure out how not to be emotional when dealing with a problem, say, "I could really use your Green...."

- If you and your spouse are discussing how to start a new business, your friends are sitting in front of the TV instead of outside taking advantage of the resort's activities and great weather, or you realize you've been way too serious about a personal issue, say, "Let's be Orange..."

Distinguished Family Members and Friends

Each Brain Color has unique ways of distinguishing their family members and friends.

- Yellow Brainers give people titles: Best Friend, Old Buddy, My Johnny.

- Blue Brainers consider their family to be their friends and their friends to be their family.

- Green Brainers are selective. They might have many acquaintances, but only a few friends.

- Orange Brainers refer to the people they do business with as their friends: My friend Carol, the nutritionist, at the health food store; All my plant pals at the Garden Center.

An Understanding Friend

Often we consider our family members our friends and our friends our family members. In her poem, "Friendship," Bessie P. Owens expresses how joyful it is to be understood, share a meaningful bond and irreplaceable acceptance.

A smile and cheerful greeting from someone on life's way;
A handclasp warm and tender, how it brightens up the day!
Just to feel that understanding when our hope's about to end,
And life is sad and weary… Oh, the joy to have a friend.

YOUR RELATIONSHIPS WITH CHILDREN

The following statistics, culled from my research projects and workshops, will help you understand your children and maintain harmony in your relationship.

Elementary Students:

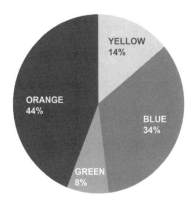

YELLOW 10%
BLUE 13%
GREEN 5%
ORANGE 72%

Middle School Students:

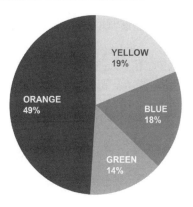

YELLOW 19%
BLUE 18%
ORANGE 49%
GREEN 14%

High School Students:

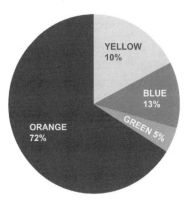

YELLOW 14%
BLUE 34%
ORANGE 44%
GREEN 8%

Adults:

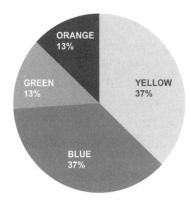

ORANGE 13%
GREEN 13%
YELLOW 37%
BLUE 37%

Brain Development

Notice that the percentage of the Orange (frontal lobe) for the elementary school students is twice that of the Yellow (temporal lobe) for adults. That contrast can significantly influence your relationship with young children.

According to Rita Carter, author of *Mapping the Mind*, "A nucleus called the reticular formation, for example, which plays a major role in maintaining attention, usually only becomes fully myelinated at or after puberty, which is why prepubescent children have a short attention span. The frontal lobe does not become fully myelinated until full adulthood. This is one reason, perhaps, why younger adults are more emotional and impulsive than those who are older."

(Note: Myelin is a sheath of white substance that acts as insulation, allowing electricity to flow swiftly and directly to sections of the brain.)

The contrast explains the frustration between Yellow Brain adults and Orange Brain children in grades K-8. However, the contrast between a Yellow Brain adult and an Orange high school student is less because children of that age have a more developed frontal lobe.

The Psychology Fair

In 1998, I facilitated a Brain Color study at the Fremd High School student psychology fair in Palatine, Illinois. The following percentages represent the 194 students who participated in the research project.

- 43% Orange: Is highly impulsive and action-oriented (% opposite adults).
- 31% Blue: Has a high level of desire to please others and gain peer approval (% similar to adults).
- 15% Yellow: Sense of responsibility and accountability for the choices they make is unusually low (% opposite of adults).
- 11% Green: Level of logical reasoning about the consequences for their actions is extremely low (% similar to adults).

The Teenage Brain

The student psychology fair statistics demonstrate why living with and working with a teenager can be tumultuous, even if you are the same Brain Color.

- A Yellow Brainer wants to have more control over his or her life than you do. "Times have changed and your rules are old fashioned."
- A Blue Brainer thinks, "You can't possibly understand my feelings and what I'm going through!"
- A Green Brainer thinks he or she is smarter than you. When our eldest son was a teen-ager, we hung a "If You Want to Know Everything, Ask a Teenager!" sign over his bedroom door.
- An Orange Brainer would be in total agreement with Katharine Hepburn: "If you obey all the rules, you miss all the fun."

I encourage you to use WCIYB to help you survive the teenage years or until your child becomes a young adult and realizes you are no longer the enemy and that you have a brain! The chart on the following page reveals your children's perspective, and offers you a guide for building and maintaining a harmonious relationship.

"Neon Orange" Angelo

Sharing WCIYB with students, their parents, and teachers in the U.S., Canada, and Europe has been a privilege and a pleasure. My heart sings each time I receive a phone call, email, or letter about how WCIYB has helped them.

My college roommate implemented the WCIYB concepts in her classroom to create a safe and respectful learning environment. Before Michelle retired, we had copious opportunities to work together and enjoy her students' Brain Colors.

The first year she used WCIYB, it was a supplementary program for her special education students and her co-worker's fourth grade class. One day, she called me to relate a story that moved both of us to tears of joy.

"When my students and I walked into the fourth grade classroom, I noticed that it had been rearranged. Angelo, an Orange Brainer, ran up

continued on page 82

A YELLOW BRAIN CHILD PERSPECTIVE

I LIKE TO: Be careful

I AM: A Leader

MY ATTITUDE IS: Follow the rules

AT SCHOOL: I assist the teacher

I LEARN BEST: When I'm prepared

AT HOME: I save my allowance

WITH MY FRIENDS: I make plans to be together

I NEED: Instructions & neatness

MY TEE SHIRT READS: "I Am Responsible and Proud"

I LIKE TO READ: History and biographies

I GET FRUSTRATED BY: Disorganization

WHEN I'M UNHAPPY: I get nervous and worry

TO ENCOURAGE ME, SAY: "I'm proud of you."

A BLUE BRAIN CHILD PERSPECTIVE

I LIKE TO: Honestly talk about my feelings

I AM: An Artist

MY ATTITUDE IS: Be cooperative

AT SCHOOL: I help my friends

I LEARN BEST WHEN: Visual aids are used

AT HOME: I like to be shown lots of love

WITH MY FRIENDS: I am a good listener

I NEED: Hugs and kisses

MY TEE SHIRT READS: "Let's Work Together"

I LIKE TO READ: Fantasy and animals stories

I GET FRUSTRATED BY: Selfishness

WHEN I'M UNHAPPY: I cry

TO ENCOURAGE ME, SAY: "I love you."

A GREEN BRAIN CHILD PERSPECTIVE

I LIKE TO: Solve problems

I AM: A Computer Wiz

MY ATTITUDE IS: Be an individual

AT SCHOOL: I'm curious and like to quietly work alone

I LEARN BEST WITH: Books and computers

AT HOME: I like my privacy and don't show my emotions

WITH MY FRIENDS: I'm a loner and don't follow the crowd

I NEED: Time to figure things out

MY TEE SHIRT READS: "It Has to Make Sense"

I LIKE TO READ: Mysteries and science fiction

I GET FRUSTRATED BY: Repetition

WHEN I'M UNHAPPY: I don't like to talk

TO ENCOURAGE ME, SAY: "I think you're smart."

AN ORANGE BRAIN CHILD PERSPECTIVE

I LIKE TO: Perform

I AM: An Athlete

MY ATTITUDE IS: Let's have fun

AT SCHOOL: I like to "do" instead of "listen"

I LEARN BEST WITH: A variety of hands-on activities

AT HOME: I like to "do my own thing"

WITH FRIENDS: I like to play games and sports

I NEED: Excitement

MY TEE SHIRT READS: "I'm a Bundle of Energy!"

I LIKE TO READ: Adventure and sports stories

I GET FRUSTRATED BY: Rules

WHEN I'M UNHAPPY: I misbehave

TO ENCOURAGE ME, SAY: "You're fun to be with."

continued from page 79

to me and said, 'Mrs. Bracken, we have a Neon Yellow substitute!' That was obvious, because the students' desks were no longer in cooperative learning groups, but in linear rows.

Since the Neon Yellow substitute had left the room, I was able to ask the class how they were doing. I learned that the children missed their teacher, an Orange/Green Brainer, and that Angelo had spent the entire morning in the hall.

'Angelo, how did it feel to spend the whole morning in the hall?' I asked.

'It was OK, because I know that I'm Neon Orange and the substitute is Neon Yellow. He's not Green and knowledgeable like Mrs. Weiss,' he boasted. Angelo, who unfortunately did not live in ideal conditions at home, knew he was safe and esteemed in his classroom, and best of all, he was proud to be Neon Orange!"

The Brain Color concept offered Angelo an opportunity to recognize and value his attributes and abilities, even if others did not. Michelle and I have never forgotten Angelo, and we hope he has never forgotten how his extraordinary his "Neon Orange" is.

Family Schedules

Families tell me they write their activities on a schedule chart or calendar using the Brain Colors. Teachers say they use the Brain Colors to post the daily or weekly activities for their students on the chalkboard.

HOME CHORES

- Yellow: Clean bedroom, take our garbage, walk the dog, or mow the lawn.
- Blue: Musical instrument practice and lessons.
- Green: Homework or school subject tutoring.
- Orange: Play dates with friends, sports practice or games, school and family vacation time.

SCHOOL SCHEDULES

- Yellow: Library time, cleaning up classroom, preparing the room for a special event.

- Blue: Music and art class or rehearsals.
- Green: Math or science class, test time, or going on an educational field trip.
- Orange: Recess, physical education class, sports practice, and vacation time.

WHAT SHOULD I WEAR TODAY?

Children, their parents, and teachers tell me that wearing a specific Brain Color t-shirt, hat, shoes, or socks at home or school visually enhances their abilities to accomplish a task.

- Yellow to be more organized about their school/home work.
- Blue to be more creative in music or art classes.
- Green to be more focused on a tests.
- Orange to have more energy for an athletic competition.

The adults say they also wear specific Brain Color clothing to help them achieve specific goals.

Brain Color Bedrooms

In Chapter 6: Thrive in Ideal Conditions, you learned to enhance your awareness of the ideal conditions in which your Brain Color thrives and be alert to changes in that environment. You can immediately recognize which Brain Color child you are observing because the condition of his bedroom reveals his Brain Color.

- Yellow Brainers: Their bedroom is immaculate. It is organized with *closed* cabinets, closets, and containers for their toys and school supplies. They get upset when an adult straightens their room when they are at school and return to find it out of order. They will get angry with their friends or siblings if they mess up *their* things and don't put them back the way they were.
- Blue Brainers: Their bedroom is a cozy place to relax, with space for imaginative play with their favorite toys. Adults often want them to clean out their collection of toys and stuffed animals because they think the child has too many, they are too old for that now, or they no longer need those things. To the child, those collections are their *friends* and they do not want to separated from or abandon their playmates.

- Green Brainers: Their bedroom is equipped with a computer, computer games, and mechanical toys. They spend a lot of time alone and do not need to play with other children. Be sure to knock and ask permission before you enter their inner sanctum. These children enjoy figuring out how things work and taking their toys apart to see what's inside. Their room often looks like a junkyard strewn with successful, almost completed, and failed experiments.

- Orange Brainers: Their bedroom is "creative chaos" where they play and work on projects that capture their attention intermittently. They *never* clean up unless an adult asks them to, or they need to find something they want. Create a game such as How Fast Can You Clean Up Your Room, and don't forget to give them a prize for their effort!

"Color-Filled" Cooperation

WCIYB is effective because it quickly imprints and resonates with children. If you want your children to be more cooperative, ask them to be:

- Yellow and clean up their room.
- Blue and help carry the groceries.
- Green and do their homework.
- Orange and plan some games for their birthday party.

An Element of Fun

In the movie *Mary Poppins*, Julie Andrews tells Michael and Jane Banks, "In every job that must be done, there is an element of fun. You find the fun and —SNAP—the job's a game!"

Using the Brain Colors will add an element of fun to your relationship with children of all ages.

SECTION II: BRAIN COLOR CONNECTIONS SUMMARY

Color Connections	Yellow Brainers	Blue Brainers	Green Brainers	Orange Brainers
Attraction to Others	Respectfulness	Thoughtfulness	Competency	Spontaneity
Why They Annoy Others	Too controlling	Overly sensitive	Intimidating & insensitive	Too unpredictable
Romantic Relationships	Serious & committed	Harmonious & affectionate	Reserved & calm	Expressive & playful
Co-Workers' Frustrations	Disorder & tardiness	Apathy & conflict	Redundancy & intrusions	Negativity & waiting
Co-Workers' Needs	Clear & detailed directions	Open discussions about issues	Cutting edge technology	Immediate results
Family Members' and Friends' Needs	Schedules & dedication	Conversations and compassion	Solitude & "no meddling"	Freedom & optimism
Children's Needs	Instructions & neatness	Hugs & kisses	Time to figure things out	Excitement & "do my own thing"

From *What Color Is Your Brain?* published by SLACK Incorporated. Copyright Sheila Glazov. www.whatcolorisyourbrain.com

SECTION III

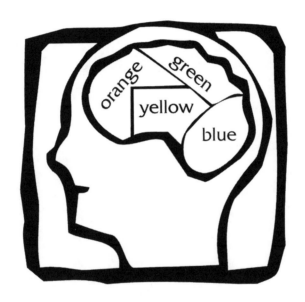

BRAIN COLOR
COMMUNICATION

11

SPEAK FLUENT BRAIN COLOR

Color is a universal language. Carl Jung, renowned for his four basic personality types said,

"Colors are the mother tongue of the subconscious."

Brain Color as a Second Language (BCSL)

When people travel to another country, they often attempt to learn the language or a few helpful phrases. However, you do not have to leave the comforts of your home to become fluent in Brain Color. Children often become fluent in Brain Color faster than adults do. However, I am confident that you can learn to speak fluent Brain Color and make it your second language.

While shopping at my favorite toy store, I was talking to the owner, who speaks fluent Brain Color. We were discussing my niece's parenting Brain Color to determine what type of birthday gifts I should purchase for her daughters.

"You're the Brain Color lady aren't you? You're Sheila Glazov!" another shopper interrupted.

"Yes, I am," I responded.

"I remember you because of your Brain Colors," she said. "We met while I was working in the children's clothing store where you had an author signing for your first book."

We had not seen each other for almost 10 years! I was amazed and delighted that she still spoke "Brain Color."

Are You Listening?

When people communicate, they consistently, and often unconsciously, tell you what color their brain is. It is easy to refine your listening skills or have fun politely eavesdropping whenever possible.

- Yellow Brainers use "**should**" and/or "**have to**" when they are talking about themselves or others.
- Blue Brainers tell you how they "**love**" or "**feel**" about something or someone.
- Green Brainers respond with, "I'll have to **think** about that."
- Orange Brainers say, "That sounds like **fun**. What are we waiting for?"

Pay Attention

If you are at a social gathering, pay attention to the conversations:

- Yellow Brainers ask about your home or the community where you live.
- Blue Brainers ask about your family and pets.
- Green Brainers ask about where you went to school, and what level of education you have.
- Orange Brainers ask about what you do for fun.

How Do You Communicate?

Whether they use a telephone call, an email, text message, letter, or invitation, each Brain Color will communicate from their perspective.

- Yellow Brainers "have to" communicate and be responsible: they will be attending the wedding.
- Blue Brainers "love to" communicate and share with others: they are going to be grandparents!
- Green Brainers "need to" communicate for a purpose: they require your code to the storage unit.
- Orange Brainers "want to" communicate something exciting: they just got a promotion and a raise.

Saying Goodbye

When concluding a telephone conversation or personally saying good-bye, you might hear:

- Yellow Brainers say, "Be careful."
- Blue Brainers say, "I love you" or "Take care."
- Green Brainers do not say anything. They have said what they had to say and just hang up the phone.
- Orange Brainers say, "Have fun!"

The "All-American" Salesman

Our youngest son is an Orange Brainer. When he became a top-level "All American" as sales representative, his sales manager wanted to know why he was so successful.

"I know what color the customer's brain is," our son said. "When I make my initial call for an appointment, I always tell the individual who referred me to him. Then I ask if I can show him the product I am selling and listen to his Brain Color response:

- The Yellow Brainers tell me they have to look at their calendar and see what their schedule is first.
- The Blue Brainers tell me all about their relationship with the person who referred me them, and say, 'I'd be happy to help you out.'
- The Green Brainers usually do not answer the phone, because they do not like to talk on the phone. But if they do answer, I tell them I am a college student, where I go to school, and why my product is so efficient.
- Orange Brainers say they are eager to see what I have, and ask, 'How soon can you come over?'"

The manager, who was also an Orange Brainer, was so eager to improve sales, he asked my son and me to facilitate workshops for the company's sales teams.

The following are our sales tips for communicating with each Brain Color.

YELLOW BRAINERS

- Be polite and punctual.
- Respect their personal values of organization and rules.
- Stay on track.
- Tell them all the details.
- Encourage them to talk about their achievements.

BLUE BRAINERS

- Show your sincerity.
- Respect their emotions.
- Use stories to explain your point.
- Connect with them personally.
- Encourage them to talk about their family.

GREEN BRAINERS

- Don't make small talk.
- Respect their privacy.
- Be brief, but informative.
- Give them lots of statistics and data.
- Encourage them to talk about their knowledge, not yours.

ORANGE BRAINERS

- Be direct.
- Respect their spontaneity.
- Make your point quickly.
- Give them the results, not facts and figures.
- Encourage them to talk about their hobbies or vacations.

Sell Your Ideas

You may not sell a product or service. However, every day you do sell your ideas to others:

- Spouses on where you would like take a vacation.
- Coworkers to stay late to help you finish a project.

- Family members to have the next holiday celebration at their house.
- Children about getting dressed and eating their breakfast on time to catch the school bus.

"You Are Speaking Green!"

In Deborah Tannen's book, *You Just Don't Understand: Women and Men in Conversaton*, she states, "We all want, above all, to be heard—but not merely to be heard. We want to be understood—heard for what we think we are saying, for what we know we meant."

Now that you know how easy it is to listen, communicate, and sell by utilizing your Brain Colors, I am confident you will quickly learn how to speak fluent Brain Color. Your fluency will enable you to communicate clearly, which will help others unmistakably hear and understand what you mean to say.

Using your Brain Color knowledge with individuals who you do not interact with on a daily basis is a valuable relationship builder. A phone conversation between a Green/Yellow computer consultant and me, a Blue/Orange Brainer, reinforced this idea.

Before we started working together, I asked the computer consultant if he would take a Brain Color Quiz. He was agreeable and eager to find out his Brain Color. I was delighted when he emailed me his results, which confirmed my hunch. He was a Green Brainer. Most Green Brainers are more adept and comfortable with technology than Blue Brainers.

I also knew it was critical to our working relationship for him to understand the Brain Color concept. During a preliminary planning conversation, I noted a change in the tone of his voice. I knew he was annoyed with the repetition of my questions.

My frustration quickly escalated. He could not grasp my confusion and need for clarification of his technical terminology. Finally, I said, "You are speaking Green and I am speaking Blue."

"I got it!" echoed through the phone.

If he had not, I am sure we would have terminated the conversation and our plans. The Brain Colors helped us establish a comfortable and compatible relationship that works.

Make It Easy

Using your Brain Color makes it easier to:

- Listen to others.
- Recognize their point of view.
- Communicate your point of view.
- Sell your ideas, product, or services.

CONNECT WITH OTHERS AND BUILD RAPPORT

Rapport is the synchronization and connection of one Brain Color's perspective with another. A prestigious and well-respected Green Brainer, an attorney (most attorneys have a high level of Green), related the following story to me.

Ladies and Gentlemen of the Jury

"I was selecting a jury in a personal injury case; I represented the plaintiff, where the claim was that the defendant was negligent and had failed to follow the proper procedure for the building of a shopping center. During jury selection, I was looking for jurors who felt that compliance with rules and regulations was significant; thus I inquired of jurors about their attitudes about dedication, service, rules, dependability, and responsibility. In other words, I was looking for those with Yellow Brain tendencies. Additionally, I wanted jurors who placed a high value on the family and the importance of a harmonious relationship; those were the Blue Brainers.

"In contrast, I was not really interested in the Green Brainers, since ultimately I was seeking money damages for the client, and I felt that the Green juror would have been far too analytical and would not attach great significance to the interruption of the life and family of the plaintiff.

"I also was not interested in the Orange Brainers because the defendants were clearly 'risk takers,' and I felt that they would be sympathetic to the defendants.

"In fact, I asked each juror to describe himself/ herself in terms such as: How do you feel about engaging in activities that present risks? Do you make plans for the future? Do you consider life to be an adventure?

What do you do for entertainment or relaxation? If I asked how you would resolve an issue, would you respond with what you think or how you feel?

"One of the jurors was a psychologist who asked me if I was using a personality profile as a guide. I gave him an affirmative response.

"Because I utilized my Brain Color knowledge, I knew I had a 'sensitive' jury that would have been favorably inclined to my facts. My adversary knew that, thus it contributed to a good settlement for my client."

Your job may not require you to pick a "sensitive" jury; however, you can use your **WCIYB** knowledge to connect with others and establish an appropriate rapport.

In Chapter 3: Appreciate Our Differences, you learned about the significant physiological, historical, and cultural interpretations of color and that you can purposefully or unconsciously respond to color because of your Brain Color. Adults, as well as children, connect with people because they are comforting, stimulating, meaningful, or memorable.

Connection Clues

The following clues will help you establish an appropriate rapport and connect with each of the Brain Colors.

YELLOW BRAINERS

- Use a diplomatic tone.
- Employ a formal approach.
- Make them feel secure.
- Understand their sense of commitment.
- Acknowledge their "follow the rules" slogan.

BLUE BRAINERS

- Use a cooperative tone.
- Employ a friendly approach.
- Make them feel appreciated.
- Understand their sensitivity.
- Acknowledge their "we can help each other" slogan.

GREEN BRAINERS

- Use an informative tone.
- Utilize an academic approach.
- Value their intelligence.
- Understand their sense of brevity.
- Acknowledge their "think it through thoroughly" slogan.

ORANGE BRAINERS

- Use an encouraging tone.
- Utilize a relaxed approach.
- Acknowledge their informal style.
- Understand their "non-traditional" sense of style.
- Acknowledge their "let's go for it!" slogan.

A Traveling Game

I find it amusing to observe and try to figure out people's Brain Colors while I wait in security lines, departure gate areas, and food courts. Travel today has become more complicated and stressful. However, you can make it "color-filled" and entertaining.

Do you remember the car traveling games, Cow Count and License Plate Search? Now, you can play the **Brain Color Connection Game**. Imagine you are at the airport and your plane is delayed for several hours. To pass the time, you decide to observe your fellow travelers and connect with them.

Brain Color Connection Game Guidelines:

- Keep an open mind. (*Under different circumstances, you may not want make a connection.*)
- Fill in the blanks with the appropriate Brain Colors.
- Write each of the Brain Colors only once in each Connection section.
- Have fun!
- Remember, it's just a game!
- Confirm your answers at the end of this chapter.

THE RIVETED READER

You cannot help noticing the man tethered to his laptop. He's definitely not the winning candidate for the *Gentleman's Quarterly* magazine cover model contest. A coffee cup, bagel bag, and *The Wall Street Journal* are a jumble of fossils beneath his seat. His over-sized, sun-dried attaché case, pregnant with technical manuals for various computers, is slumped in the seat between you. If you began to choke on your snack, he would not even notice. However, if in your distress, you flung yourself over his mountain of reading material, you would capture his attention. He would administer an effective Heimlich maneuver, and return to his work unfazed.

Your Brain Color Connection

The Riveted Reader is a _____ Brainer. You connect with him because you are a:

1. _____ Brainer and laugh because his jumble of fossils reminds you of your office.

2. _____ Brainer and you have similar reading material in your briefcase.

3. _____ Brainer and he reminds you of your favorite uncle.

3. _____ Brainer and you should tell him that the flight is boarding and the gate has been changed.

MS. FRAN FRIENDLY

You are waiting for your flight to board. The woman sitting next to you is wearing a Halloween sweater with black cats and orange pumpkin appliqués that match her earrings. A charm bracelet with pictures of her children dressed in their soccer uniforms adorns her wrist. She asks you if you are traveling on business or pleasure. You tell her you are going home and she responds with a recitation of her entire family dossier. In only a few minutes, you know each of her family members by name, including their pets. Then she offers an apology and says, "I've been such a chatterbox, I haven't given you an opportunity to tell me about yourself."

Your Brain Color Connection

Ms. Fran Friendly is a _____ Brainer. You connect with her because you are a:

1. _____ Brainer and a freelance sportswriter compiling research for an article about soccer moms.

2. _____ Brainer and feel like you and a long-lost friend were reunited.

3. _____ Brainer and interested in sharing your vital statistics and family history and offer to exchange email addresses and phone numbers to stay in touch.

4. _____ Brainer and amused by the reruns of "This Is Your Life, Fran Friendly."

A CROCODILE COWBOY BIKER

On the way to an empty seat, you almost stumble over a pair of crocodile, silver-tipped cowboy boots. An eccentric looking gentleman apologizes, stands up and invites you to sit down next to him. He is wearing a caramel toffee-colored deerskin-fringed jacket and cowboy hat trimmed with spotted snakeskin, a bleached lizard jaw, and delicate quail feathers. Before you can answer, he tells you, "I'm traveling on business, but I'm always havin' fun!" Then he regales you with his stories as an attorney, a real estate developer, a private pilot, and a Harley rider.

Your Brain Color Connection

The Crocodile Cowboy Biker is a _____ Brainer. You connect with him because you are a:

1. _____ Brainer and accept a silver-embossed business card because he could be a valuable business connection in the future.

2. _____ Brainer and also ride a Harley and want to purchase a 1970s muscle car.

3. _____ Brainer and know he is a quick course in entrepreneurship, which could be useful after 25 years in corporate America.

4. _____ Brainer and are inspired and entertained by his stories.

THE MARTHA STEWART OF THE MIDWEST

You sit down next to a woman who looks like a senior model for a Ralph Lauren line of clothing. She is impeccably dressed; her cordovan loafers have a military gloss and she is reading *The Clutter Busting*

Handbook. You decide to ask her why she is traveling and she answers, "I just spent three weeks helping my youngest daughter and her family move into their new home. Now I'm returning home to Iowa City."

Your Brain Color Connection

The Martha Stewart of the Midwest is a _____ Brainer. You connect with her because you are a:

1. _____ Brainer and find her a pleasure. You tell her that her family is fortunate to have such a talented mother and grand-mother.

2. _____ Brainer and intrigued by her wealth of knowledge, which sounds like a "moving day" version of the *Gettysburg Address.*

3. _____ Brainer and know you need to learn more about her Extreme Nanny Techniques for Disciplining Toddlers and Teenagers.

4. _____ Brainer and are ready to take an Advanced Placement Class for Helpful Household Hints for the Working Woman.

Now, you can enjoy playing the **Brain Color Connection Game** wherever you are: at a holiday cocktail party, commuter train station, business conference "meet 'n greet," or while you are traveling. You will find your observations and your connections with others entertaining instead of aggravating.

Your Brain Color Connection Answers:

- The Riveted Reader is a Green Brainer. You connect with him because you are:

  1. Orange
  2. Green
  3. Blue
  4. Yellow

- Ms. Fran Friendly is a Blue Brainer. You connect with her because you are:

  1. Green
  2. Blue
  3. Yellow
  4. Orange

- The Crocodile Cowboy Biker is an Orange Brainer. You connect with him because you are:

  1. Green
  2. Orange
  3. Yellow
  4. Blue

- The Martha Stewart of the Midwest is a Yellow Brainer. You connect with her because you are:

  1. Blue
  2. Green
  3. Orange
  4. Yellow

No-Brainer Conflict Resolution

Frosty the Snowman

I arrived home late one evening after a business dinner. When I entered the back hall, I felt like I had opened the door to my butcher's walk-in freezer. As I walked into the family room, I thought Frosty the Snowman was watching the football game on our couch. I knew it was best to leave my husband alone. As I left the room, I almost tripped on the edge of the area rug when I heard him say, "I didn't know where you were."

"I called you at the office and I told you my schedule," I responded.

I pressed my fingers to my lips to keep from smiling, when my husband stabbed the TV control button off and said, "It's almost 10 o'clock, I was really getting concerned."

"I appreciate your concern, darling," I said, snuggling up next to him. "However, this isn't really about me, it's *really* about your Green. You didn't know where I was, you couldn't call anyone and tell them you were concerned about me, because you didn't remember what I told you this morning. You were focused on what you were doing. In other words, you felt stupid and Green people never want to feel stupid."

I could feel my "Frosty" defrosting. "We could argue about this or be Blue," I said.

We were able to defuse an upset and resolve a conflict without blame or an argument. We changed the situation and averted a conflict with understanding and humor, because we knew each other's Brain Color.

The following chart will help you:

- interpret signals when you or someone else is having an "off color" day.
- decrease your internal and external conflicts.
- increase the compatibility in your relationships.

Misunderstandings

Miscommunications create misunderstandings. Learning how to communicate and interpret in Brain Color will reduce conflicts and increase harmony in your life.

Planning a wedding is known to be one of the most stressful and joyful times in a person's life. The type or size of one's budget, family, and venue often creates conflict. The following bridal couple quotes communicate possible bumps in the road on the way to their wedding celebration.

- A Yellow Brainer bride says, "But I have dreamed and planned for this type of wedding all my life."
- A Blue Brainer groom says, "Why can't we invite all my friends, including my wrestling coach?"
- A Green Brainer bride says, "I want it to be a small gathering, just family and a few close friends."
- An Orange Brainer groom says, "A destination wedding, on our favorite beach in Hawaii, would be fantastic!"

Engaged couples who deal with their own opinions and emotions, as well as parents, officiates, wedding planners, and vendors can benefit from the following no-brainer conflict resolution verse:

Greens never want to be wrong and
Yellows always need be right.
Blues continue to talk and talk, while
Oranges need to take a hike.

NO-BRAINER CONFLICT RESOLUTION

Brain Color Conflict	*Brain Color Compatibility*
Yellow Conflict	**Yellow Compatibility**
Is judgmental and self-righteous	Takes care of others
Becomes controlling	Completes tasks
Complains and expresses self-pity	Is prompt
Demonstrates inflexibility	Committed to work/home
Worries about the future	Knows what is expected
Blue Conflict	**Blue Compatibility**
Cries and becomes hysterical	Gets and gives hugs
Becomes depressed and remorseful	Enjoys and respects nature
Says "I'm fine," but really isn't	Is compassionate and truthful
Does not face reality	Shares feelings openly
Acts irrationally	Trusts intuition
Green Conflict	**Green Compatibility**
Gives others the cold shoulder	Utilizes knowledge
Becomes sarcastic and critical	Satisfies curiosity
Shows indifference and insensitivity	Is competent and precise
Is uncooperative	Follows a system or method
Pouts	Promotes justice and fairness
Orange Conflict	**Orange Compatibility**
Acts immaturely and is belligerent	Demonstrates skillfulness
Becomes disobedient, breaks rules	Competes with others
Is rude and physically aggressive	Is courageous and takes risks
Drops out physically and emotionally	Enjoys life's challenges
Shows compulsive behavior	Expresses themselves freely

The Back Story

As in a book or movie, if you get to know and understand another person's back story, you can reduce misunderstandings and miscommunications. Their back story contains all the relevant events or circumstances that have influenced their point of view and behavior. Stop, think, and appreciate the fact that others may not know how or want to do things the way you would.

Misunderstandings and conflict make it difficult for individuals to appreciate their differences. The result: they become "Shadowed" and demonstrate the unconscious negative or dark side of their personality.

When explaining this concept to children, I tell them that a Shadowed individual is a "Meevillain." When you become a Meevillain, the focus is on "Me." You can be tempted to do "evil" things, and then become a "villain" to others and yourself. Meevillain offers the children an amusing way to explain Shadowed behavior. I tell them that when they have Meevillain behavior, their attitude about themselves and others changes. They become less understanding of other people's differences. Where there had once been open acceptance and respect for others, they build walls of mistrust and misunderstanding.

During an author school visit, students related their Meevillain stories to me.

- "In the morning, when my mom's in a hurry get to work, she can be a Yellow Meevillain."
- "When my sister's boyfriend doesn't call her, she freaks out and becomes a Blue Meevillain."
- "I tell my brother he is a Green Meevillain when he won't play video games with me."
- "When my friend loses a soccer game, he's a total Orange Meevillain."

You Can Ask in Color

To avoid becoming a Meevillain and easily resolve conflict, utilize your Brain Colors. Ask the other person to become more of another Brain Color.

- To get a job done on time, ask an Orange Brainer to be more Yellow.
- For more affection or compassion from a Green Brainer, ask him to be more Blue.
- For some quiet time to solve a problem, ask a Blue Brainer to be more Green.
- To close a sale, ask a Yellow Brainer to be more Orange.

These examples demonstrate how to eliminate criticism and conflict and create compatibility by speaking Brain Color.

External and Internal Conflict

Different Brain Color perspectives create external and internal conflict and incompatibility.

- A Yellow Brainer's ideal classroom requires strict discipline, but creates more friction with his Orange Brainer students who have a robust aversion to the rules.
- A Blue Brainer wants to discusss staff problems, but creates additional tension with her Green Brainer manager, who feels she should solve the problems herself.
- A Green Brainer remains calm during a family crisis; however, her Blue emotions tug at her heart and cause conflict with other family members.
- An Orange Brainer's desire to own a small business motivates him; however, his Yellow sense of responsibility for employees and record keeping frustrate him.

Wet Paint

When our Brain Color intensifies, compatibility can be problematic. Yellow is the most intense color of the color spectrum and the most intense personality to work with. However, I think the following advice from my friend's mother, who was a Yellow Brainer, is intensely wise: "When you're in the midst of conflict, tell yourself or others, I'm Wet Paint! I need time to dry!"

14

You Can Change Your Brain Color

"Do we always remain the same colors or does our Brain Color change?" is a question I am often asked. "Yes, you can change your Brain Color," is my answer. You can purposefully change your Brain Color or be motivated to change by circumstances you have no control over.

A Green Brainer had worked in the corporate world for 25 years. A company merger required him to choose a new career path. "This is the business opportunity I'm going to take advantage of," he told his wife. "I no longer have to play it safe and be concerned about a steady income; our family is grown and you wanted to take an early retirement. I can start and run a business better than the people I used to work for."

The Green Brainer enjoyed his new Orange Brain freedom. He ran his business as he pleased. No Yellow mandates and Blue management meetings with the other people. However, after three years, his business had taken on a life of its own. It required additional employees and a structured business environment. His solution was to hire an administrative assistant to handle the Yellow and Blue parts of his successful enterprise.

Your Brain and Change

Each of the Brain Colors handles change from their own perspective.

- Yellow Brainers must *plan* for change. To be comfortable, they need to feel they are in control of the change.
- Blue Brainers must *feel* good about a change. To be comfortable, they need to trust their intuition about the change.
- Green Brainers must *think* about change. To be comfortable, they need to gather and contemplate all the facts before they consider making a change.

- Orange Brainers *are* the "change agents." To be comfortable, they constantly need to create change. They cannot stand boredom.

Family Changes

Changes in the framework of the 21st century family have created diverse opportunities and challenges. WCIYB can help you deal more effectively with the changes you experience while raising your children or taking care of your parents.

As a Blue/Orange Brainer, I fell in love with my husband's Orange/Green Brainer attributes and abilities. However, after our children were born, my husband became a Neon Orange fun father. To bring a sense of order to the framework of our family, I transformed myself into a Yellow/Blue "by-the-rule book" mother.

Early in our marriage, my husband's Orange ideas and independent behavior often irritated my mother's Neon Yellow sense of propriety. However, eventually, she rode on his motorcycle and he went to her country club.

Through the years, my husband and my mother grew to trust, understand, value, and love one another. This was evident and invaluable when my mother was in hospice care before her death. It was a gift watching my husband and mother transform again. He changed his Brain Color to Blue and she changed hers to Green.

His compassion for her was unequaled, and she realized that it made sense to allow us to be responsible for her care and execute her wishes. Those Brain Color changes gave my mother, me, my husband, and our family the gifts of love, laughter, joy, and comfort as we all experienced my mother's passing and celebration of her life.

Life Changes

Life experiences and maturity offer us opportunities and conditions to change our Brain Colors.

- Yellow Brainers become more Orange. They do not have to be as responsible to their family, careers, or community as they did when they were younger. With their children grown, they feel it's their time to have new adventures. They have the resources and the time to do "crazy" things and become risk-takers.

- Green Brainers become more Blue. They do not have to be focused on solving business or family problems. They have amassed a life-time of knowledge and experience, but no longer need to impart it to others. They have opportunities to show the sensitive Blue facet of their personality.

- Blue Brainers become more Green. They no longer have to nurture others. They can be self-caring and focus on themselves. They take good care of themselves by going back to school, focusing on a new career, or delving into a hobby that earlier required too much time or money.

- Orange Brainers become more Yellow. They actually become tired of taking risks and want more security. They are comfortable not being the "crazies" in their family or circle of friends. While they still like to march to a different drummer, they change their brisk tempo to a slower pace.

Environmental Changes

Environment can influence you to change your Brain Color. One of the nation's largest office supply companies hired me to facilitate a workshop. As I entered the lobby, my Yellow Brain began to shift to Blue. A color-ful decor and pictorial history of the company greeted me as I walked toward a large cafeteria, which faced a landscaped garden adjacent to my destination. The meeting room had a gallery of employees with smiling faces. The color scheme was teal and cranberry accented by soft lighting. Upholstered chairs surrounded the tables, which allowed the attendees to make eye contact during the workshop. It was a comfortable and comfort-ing environment, which enhanced the attendees' attention and ability to learn new skills.

 ### YELLOW BRAINERS CAN CHANGE IN A:
- Yellow, well-organized situation.
- Blue situation that encourages a traditional, family-type atmosphere.
- Green situation that maintains systematic routine.
- Orange situation that has a game plan.

BLUE BRAINERS CAN CHANGE IN A:

- Blue environment that is friendly.
- Yellow environment that has day care for their children.
- Green environment that appreciates their authenticity.
- Orange environment that acknowledges their social contributions to the group.

GREEN BRAINERS CAN CHANGE IN A:

- Green setting that is efficient.
- Yellow setting that values consistent quality.
- Blue setting with smart people.
- Orange "virtual" setting that requires no meetings.

ORANGE BRAINERS CAN CHANGE IN A:

- Orange climate that is stimulating and high-spirited.
- Yellow climate that provides an opportunity for physical activity.
- Green climate that values direct responses.
- Blue climate that encourages imagination.

A Challenge

Whenever a life experience or changing my Brain Color has challenged me, I encourage myself with one of my favorite affirmations:

"It was gruesome and I grew some. In fact, I should be 10 feet tall by now."

EFFECTIVE DECISION MAKING

"It's not hard to make decisions when you know what your values are."
—Roy Disney

Knowing your Brian Colors makes it easier to recognize your values and make decisions. Every day, we confront issues and make decisions that are stressful and can affect our health. My family knows all too well how stress affects individuals and their families who live with the daily challenges of a chronic disease. My father had Type II diabetes, and our son, Joshua, was diagnosed with Type I diabetes in 1985, when he was 15 years old.

Stress has a tremendous effect on blood sugar levels and diabetes management. The following vignettes demonstrate how relationships can create stress, especially when the individuals are not aware of each other's Brain Colors and what they value.

Blue and Green Brain Stress

A wife thinks she is being thoughtful when she asks her husband how his blood sugar levels have been. He tells her, "Second-guessing my diabetes management is unnecessary; you should know I'm not stupid. I can take care of myself!"

"You don't appreciate me," she sobs. "It takes time to shop, prepare, and cook all the appropriate foods for you, and you don't even notice!"

The husband ignores his wife and retreats to his garage workshop to tinker with his motorcycle.

If the wife knew her husband was a Green Brainer, she would have understood his need for privacy and sense of competency about his diabetes management. If the husband knew his wife was a Blue Brainer, he would have recognized that she asked him about his diabetes because she wanted to be helpful and demonstrate her love and concern for his well-being. Their Brain Color knowledge would have reinforced their appreciation for each other's values and attitudes, and shown them how they each could contribute to the husband's diabetes management.

Yellow and Orange Stress

A father thinks he is doing the right thing when he decides to tells his teenage daughter, "I know what is best for you; you *must* keep a detailed record of your meals, exercise, and glucose levels in your logbook."

His daughter says, "I'm furious with *you*, *your* rules, and *your* intrusion in *my* life." Then she stomps off to her room, slams the door, and calls her best friend to complain about her father, "who treats me like a baby!"

If the father knew his daughter was an Orange Brainer, it would have reinforced the fact that Orange teenagers are highly impulsive and loathe parental lectures. If the daughter recognized that her father was a Yellow Brainer, she would know he needed to be a responsible parent and coach her about a game plan to manage her diabetes. Their Brain Color knowledge would have helped them be receptive to each other's values and attitudes.

The chart on the facing page will help you reflect on your decision-making process during stressful or tranquil times in your life.

"We're Going to Die!"

Effective decision making was crucial for saving lives, on the ground and in the air, when my husband, Jordan, and I managed the county airport and operated a commuter airline in the Sierra Nevada mountains. One day, Jordan, who professionally is a Green/Orange Brainer, was piloting our commuter airplane to Los Angeles. As he retracted the landing gear, one of the passengers noticed oil spewing from the right engine and screamed, "We're going to die, we're going to die!"

BRAIN COLOR EFFECTIVE DECISION MAKING

Yellow Brain Effective Decision Making

Create a detailed plan

Think through all ideas

Execute in a timely manner

Do not procrastinate

"Go by the book."

Consider the cost

Blue Brain Effective Decision Making

Use their heart not their head

Talk to about idea(s) with others

Seek out other people's input

"I've got to go with my intuition."

Think how it affects others

Money is not the issue

Green Brain Effective Decision Making

Research and analyze data

Calculate risks/downside

Applying formulas

Create systems

Project outcomes

Evaluate financial ramifications

Orange Brain Effective Decision Making

Be in the moment

Improvise

Look at competition

Ignore the fear

No thought of consequences

"If you've got the money, use it."

"Madam, if you do not stop screaming, we *are* going to die!" Jordan warned, as his Yellow Brain executed the emergency checklist procedures. His directive quieted the passenger while he circled back to the airport and safely landed the airplane. My husband's Yellow Brain flight training and Orange Brain calm in a crisis let the passengers know he was in control and they were *not* going to die.

Golda My Dear

I know from my own personal experiences that WCIYB is helpful when you have to make decisions about the people and the pets you love.

Over the years, our family has loved and enjoyed numerous cats and dogs. However, my beloved companion was our Golden/Newfoundland/Labrador, Golda My Dear. When I noticed Golda had an unusual cough,

I made an appointment to see our veterinarian. After several x-rays and extensive lab work, Dr. Hinkle said, "Golda has lung cancer."

The diagnosis shoved my heart through a paper shredder. Then Dr. Hinkle, a Green/Blue Brainer who was familiar with the Brain Color concept, said, "Rainbow Lady, I know this is terribly hard for you, you are so Blue. Go home and be Green. Think about what you want to do for Golda."

His comforting words helped me navigate the road home. I knew I had to remain calm. I could not become hysterical and cause an accident that would endanger us or someone else. By the time we arrived home, I had shifted my Blue to Green. I commenced my research, encouraged myself to be resourceful, and strategized a hospice plan for Golda.

After two weeks of making Golda as comfortable as possible, I realized we had to make that final appointment with Dr. Hinkle. It was an excruciating decision. However, knowing I had done my best gave me peace in my heart and my head.

These challenging experiences reinforced an invaluable lesson: No matter what your Brain Color, you can purposely shift to another Brain Color to solve even the most difficult problems.

Motivate Your Brain

If you are motivated to shift your Brain Color, you can successfully change your behavior, effectively make decisions, resolve conflicts, and reduce the stress in your life. To motivate yourself or others you need to understand the appropriate Brain Color motivators.

 ### YELLOW BRAINER MOTIVATORS

- Doing what is right
- Completing a to-do list
- Deadlines
- Respect
- Symbolic recognition

BLUE BRAINER MOTIVATORS

- Others listening to and valuing my ideas
- Opportunities to share my feelings
- Not being taken for granted
- A pat on the back
- Creative opportunities

GREEN BRAINER MOTIVATORS

- Problem-solving opportunities
- Creating a system or procedure
- Feedback at the end of a project
- Cutting edge resources
- Recognition of my solution

ORANGE BRAINER MOTIVATORS

- Thrill of a new challenge
- Financial rewards
- Rapid results
- Competition
- The excitement of change

The Clarity of Confusion

Confusion is a powerful motivator and influences our decision-making process, if we are willing to be uncomfortable and patient. Many years ago, a Green Brainer friend offered me advice: "Sit with confusion like a brick in your lap." His wisdom taught me a valuable lesson that I have not forgotten and that I share with others: *out of confusion comes clarity.*

16

CELEBRATE HASSLE-FREE HOLIDAYS

"When our relatives are at home, we have to think of all their good points or it would be impossible to endure them."
—George Bernard Shaw

Relative Celebrations

When your relatives come home for a holiday or a special occasion, do you think they resemble the people on a Disney World dream vacation brochure or the "most wanted" listings at your local post office?

You can enjoy your relatives and those celebrations with less stress, the appropriate gifts, and more time for fun if you understand the Brain Colors of everyone involved, including your own.

The following chart is a holiday gift to you and your family. Down the left side you will see a list of activities, traditions, and emotions associated with the holidays. Across the chart to the right, you will see how each of the Brain Colors interprets or associates with the activities, traditions, and emotions. You will:

- understand that Uncle Al, a Green Brainer, is not the curmudgeon you thought he was.
- appreciate Cousin Marilyn's Yellow Brainer ability to purchase *the* perfect gift for *each* member of your family.
- find it easy to buy a gift for Aunt Sylvia, a Blue Brainer, who loves collecting family photos.
- know why your Orange Brainer friend, JB, will be thrilled with a pictorial book about hiking the Himalayas.

The holiday and celebration tips that follow will help you put the holiday spirit back in your celebrations.

CELEBRATE HASSLE-FREE HOLIDAYS

Holiday/ Celebration Tips	Yellow Brainers	Blue Brainers	Green Brainers	Orange Brainers
Joys	Customs	Family & friends	Alone time	Entertainment
Stressors	Last-minute changes	No offers to help	Hustle & bustle	Obligations
Shopping	Makes list	Makes gifts	Shops online	Last minute
Holiday quotes	"Tradition! Tradition!"	"I just called to say I love you"	"Bah, humbug"	"Let's party"
Enjoyable activities	Annual holiday favorites	Sit and talk with family & friends	Put toys & games together	Play games & sports
Decorating the house	Organized & same as last year	Creative & handmade	A system for how best to do it	Can't remember where stuff is
Gatherings	Timely	Relaxed	Quiet	Noisy
Gifts	Practical: Clocks, watches, purses, robes, sweaters, scarves, jewelry, picture album, wallet, calendar	Romantic: Picture frames, candles, garden items, gifts for pets, tickets to a play or concert	Technical: Cutting edge gadgets, computers, electronic devices, lessons, books	Fun: Sports equipment or memorabilia, tools, gadgets, tickets to a sporting event or getaway trip

continued

CELEBRATE HASSLE-FREE HOLIDAYS

Flowers	Traditional flowers in attractive, reusable container	Colorful flowers they can arrange themselves	A plant they don't have to care for	A variety of flowers and colorful balloons
Books	History, bestsellers, religion	Biography, self-help, inspirational	Technology, mysteries, crossword puzzles	Sports, "how to...", adventures

Bonus Gifts

If you implement the holiday and celebration tips, you will also receive the following bonus gifts:

- Assist a Yellow Brainer and help him plan the next family get-together. You will win a "respectable" 1st place ribbon.
- Score points with a Blue Brainer. Give her a "love gift" when it is *not* a holiday or special occasion.
- Give the Green Brainers a little extra solitude and they will *not* mumble "Bah, humbug!" at your celebration.
- Delight your Orange Brainer with a "How did you do it?" or "It's exactly what I wanted!" gift.

Expectations and Frustrations

Frustration can be a consequence for having expectations about a holiday, family celebration, or a special event.

- Yellow Brainers expect everything to go according to their plan and become frustrated when it does not. A Yellow Brainer learned to calm and comfort herself with the old expression, "When man makes plans, God laughs." However, it was not a laughing matter when her holiday party caterer was two hours late. She was tempted to fire him, but asked herself: "Do I want to be right or be happy?"

- Blue Brainers are non-confrontational and expect others to understand why they are being emotional about a situation. It was the first year empty nesters did not have any of their children at home to celebrate Christmas. The wife was annoyed because her husband did not understand why she was not in the "holiday spirit," and the husband was irritated because he thought his wife was overreacting.

- Green Brainers do not give or get enough information from others. However, they expect the people who know them best to be mind-readers. A workaholic was frustrated because her husband and children did not understand why she became absorbed in her work, forgot to call home, and was late to their annual Halloween pumpkin-carving party.

- Orange Brainers expect to have fun and are disappointed when they do not. A young man was looking forward to his family reunion at their favorite ski resort. At the last minute, his cousin had to cancel. He expressed his upset by telling his cousin, "I understand, but jumping off of a cornice and skiing the back bowls of the mountain just won't be as much fun without you."

Why Do You Do It That Way?

You might think other Brain Colors' behaviors are unusual because they handle holidays or special occasions differently. However, their actions might keep them from feeling overwhelmed or disappointed and create relief or enjoyment.

- A week before a dinner party, a Yellow Brainer planned which games her dinner guests would play, set her dinner table and arranged the place cards, organized all the food platters on her kitchen counter according to when they needed to be prepared, and wrote a to-do list for herself and her husband.

- A Blue Brainer told me that one of her greatest joys is hosting a Thanksgiving dinner for her entire family. When a new family member said, "Maybe next year we will have our own celebration," she was devastated and immediately expressed her disappointment. However, other family members reassured her that they *would* be celebrating at her house again next year.

- A Green Brainer always volunteered to be the bartender or chef for the neighborhood Fourth of July party. He liked to mix the drinks or grill the burgers as requested, and not have to make small talk with the other neighbors, especially the ones he did not know or like.

- Sorting all the Chanukah gifts into separate piles for each family member was a delight for the Orange Brainer. He also enjoyed orchestrating his "one at a time" gift opening ritual and directing the spectators in a chorus of "ooh's" and "aah's" as each adult and child opened a gift and became the center of everyone's attention.

A Gift of Change

If you do something thoughtful for someone who is going through or has been through a challenging time, he or she will appreciate your kindness and enjoy the gifts change can offer.

Our niece, a Green/Blue Brainer, is the hostess for our annual Glazov family Chanukah party. However, one year she called everyone to ask if we would be upset if she changed the format of our celebration. We all encouraged her to do what worked best for her, and she promised to reinstate our traditional celebration the next year.

We celebrated with snacks, my traditional Chanukah cookies, and latkes from the grocery store instead of the usual homemade latkes. The family agreed that being together for a hassle-free celebration was more important than who made the latkes.

Celebrating Change

During the holidays, change and stress can be significant. In Chapter 14: You Can Change Your Brain Color, you learned that each of the Brain Colors handles change from their own perspective.

Missing a loved one who has passed away can be a stressful change during the holiday season or a family celebration. John De Berry, a grief counselor and consultant who was the Bereavement Coordinator of Palliative Care and Home Hospice Program at Chicago's Northwestern Memorial Hospital says, "Change is inevitable; growth is optional. We need to acknowledge our unique differences and understand that we may not act as we did when everyone in the family was together. Changes can create growth if we focus on the positive in people. For the first set of holidays, you can blend aspects of the past with the present."

Creating a remembrance or legacy can be comforting and ease stress:

- A Yellow Brainer could establish a remembrance tradition with a special prayer or by serving a loved one's favorite food at a celebration or holiday meal.

- A Blue Brainer may enjoy sharing stories about a loved one or singing his or her favorite holiday songs, especially with the adults and children who did not know the person.

- A Green Brainer may want to observe a private memorial to honor a loved one by visiting the cemetery or lighting a remembrance candle.

- An Orange Brainer might like to celebrate a loved one's life and memory by releasing balloons that contain a "love" message or engaging in a loved one's favorite sport or hobby.

Moving On

Expectations, change, and stress often keep us from enjoying the moment and moving on to celebrate our lives in a new way. Author Victor Parachin says, *"We can use the past as a guide post or a hitching post."*

HELPFUL CLUES AND QUOTES

My Green/Blue accountant likes to say, "I went through life doing and saying things, but not knowing why. I'm no longer color blind; the Brain Colors cured me and gave me the answers too!"

With the following collection of Brain Color quotes and clues, you will be able to recognize other Brain Colors when you meet or interact with them at home, at work, or in your community. Just for fun, I have included a list of famous people, their careers, and what I propose is their appropriate Brain Color according to my research and the **WCIYB** concepts.

Yellow Brainer Quotes and Clues

- "The baby was born at the wrong time; it messed up my schedule during the big selling season."
- "I come in a half hour before work to stock towels, fill our receipt book with totals, and enter them into the computer."
- "I can't stand the money not facing up; it all should be facing the same way!"
- "Yellow people are 'T' crossers and 'I' dotters."
- "I'm Rependable! That means I'm respectful and dependable." (I promised, Eric, a fifth grader, I would always give him credit when I used his word.)
- "I organize, supervise, delegate, follow up, and reinforce."

YELLOW BRAINERS

- forward "neatnik tips" to friends and family.
- are worriers. You *do not have* to worry; they are worrying for you.
- often seem rushed; their need to stay on schedule and complete everything on their to-do list is a priority.
- find it hard to control their urge to straighten pictures on a restaurant wall, lampshades in the hotel lobby, or decorative pillows on a friend's living room sofa.

FAMOUS YELLOW BRAINERS

- President George Washington
- General Colin Powell
- Prime Minister Margaret Thatcher
- Emily Post, etiquette expert
- Sam Walton, founder of Wal-mart

Blue Brainer Quotes and Clues

- "I love you more than tongue can tell!"
- "Every year when new interns arrive, we give them the Brain Color quiz and explain how we use this in the agency."
- "I need a real person! I don't want to talk to a tech person or go to a website."
- "My friends are the people who know the songs in my heart, and sing them to me when I forget the words."
- "It's easy to speak my mind, because it comes from straight from my heart."

BLUE BRAINERS

- leave "love notes" in their loved ones' lunch bags, suitcases, kitchen cabinets, or briefcases.
- want peace at any price; however, they usually pay a huge price.

- can drive themselves as well as others crazy (especially the Green Brainers) when they reiterate their issue of concern or idea repeatedly while trying to solve a problem.
- expect people to be nice and are disappointed when they aren't.

FAMOUS BLUE BRAINERS

- President Abraham Lincoln
- Mother Teresa
- Martin Luther King, Jr.
- First Lady Eleanor Roosevelt
- Robert Frost, poet

Green Brainer Quotes and Clues

- "I'm glad my kids are smart, because I would not have tolerated it if they were dumb."
- "I wish everyone would stop bothering me."
- "Word count for this issue is 5,114 words – total read time about 15 minutes."
- "I need to know that, why? And it affects me, how?"
- "Anytime I can solve a problem, it's a good day!"
- "I don't need to know what doesn't pertain to me; the less I know about others, the better."

GREEN BRAINERS

- do not have to like or have a relationship with others in order to work with them.
- want to get all the facts from other people, but they don't give the facts to others: "We don't want them to know what we know; we want to know what they know."
- are proficient at remembering data: dates, numbers, years, places, and facts. They are big winners at Trivial Pursuit.
- like people to come to them with questions, but can be condescending with the answers.

FAMOUS GREEN BRAINERS

- President Thomas Jefferson
- Frank Lloyd Wright
- Dr. Jonas Salk
- Bill Gates
- Thomas Edison

Orange Brainer Quotes and Clues

- "I can pretty much do anything, so you can carry on and be brilliant!"
- "I am not being belligerent!"
- "Just fly the airplane!"
- "I don't have to explain my behavior—they have to explain theirs."
- "I've worked in the ER for 23 years!"

ORANGE BRAINERS

- look at life as a verb, not a noun.
- don't want details; just give them the bottom line.
- think if they obey all the rules, they will miss all the fun.
- don't want to be paralyzed by policies.

FAMOUS ORANGE BRAINERS

- President Bill Clinton
- Lee Iacocca
- Prime Minister Golda Meir
- Amelia Earhart
- John Glenn, astronaut

SECTION III: BRAIN COLOR COMMUNICATION SUMMARY

Color Communication	Yellow Brainers	Blue Brainers	Green Brainers	Orange Brainers
Communication Style	Be polite Stay on track Tell them details	Show your sincerity Use stories Connect personally	No "small talk" Be brief Give statistics	Be direct Quick to the point Give results
Tone of Voice	Diplomatic	Cooperative	Informative	Encouraging
Approach With Others	Formal	Friendly	Academic	Relaxed
Encourages	Commitment	Sensitivity	Brevity	Spontaneity
Slogans	"Follow the rules"	"We can help each other"	"Think it through, thoroughly"	"Let's go for it"
Listen, They Say	"Should"	"Love"	"Think"	"Fun"
Ask About Your	Home & community	Family & pets	Education	Hobbies
Telephone Goodbyes	"Be careful"	"I love you" or "Take care"	Don't say anything; they just hang up	"Have fun"

continued

From *What Color Is Your Brain?* published by SLACK Incorporated. Copyright Sheila Glazov. www.whatcolorisyourbrain.com

SECTION III: BRAIN COLOR COMMUNICATION SUMMARY

Color Communication	Yellow Brainers	Blue Brainers	Green Brainers	Orange Brainers
Compatible Behavior	Completes tasks Cares for others Knows expectations	Enjoys nature Shares feelings Shows compassion	Satisfies curiosity Is precise Promotes justice	Is skillful Enjoys competition Is courageous
Conflict Behavior	Judgmental Inflexible Complains	Remorseful Unrealistic Irrational	Sarcastic Critical Uncooperative	Impulsive Disobedient Aggressive
Change	Plan for it	Feel good about it	Think about it	Do it
Decision Making	Conventional	Consults with others	Projects outcomes	Takes action
Holiday Celebrations	"Tradition! Tradition!"	"I just called to say I love you"	"Bah, humbug"	"Let's party"
Clues and Quotes	"Yellow people are T crossers and I dotters" "It messed up my schedule"	"I love you more than tongue can tell" "I need to talk to a real person"	"I wish everyone would stop bothering me" "I'm glad my kids are smart"	"I can pretty much do anything!" "I am not being belligerent"
Famous People	George Washington Colin Powell Sam Walton	Abraham Lincoln Mother Theresa Martin Luther King, Jr.	Thomas Jefferson Thomas Edison Bill Gates	Bill Clinton Amelia Earhart Lee Iacocca

From *What Color Is Your Brain?* published by SLACK Incorporated. Copyright Sheila Glazov. www.whatcolorisyourbrain.com

EPILOGUE

My Blue Brainer perspective views a celebration as a beginning, not an ending. Yes, this is the ending of the book. However, it is the beginning of your "Brainday" celebrations and you are the guest of honor. Congratulations!

You have learned the fundamental Brain Color concepts: how to understand and value yourself and others, resolve conflicts quickly, build harmonious relationships, and improve your job performance. I encourage you to continue honoring yourself and celebrating your Yellow, Blue, Green, and Orange Brainer strengths and perspectives. They are color-filled gifts you can share with others and use in every facet of your life.

Have fun being who you are! Think about your Brainday as a birthday, which by definition is a day commemorating the founding or beginning of something. Unlike a traditional once-a-year birthday, you can celebrate your Brainday every day!

I feel blessed to have an abundance of Brainday and birthday memories. One of my favorite memories is our youngest son's sixth birthday party. Noah celebrated as the ringmaster of twelve guests, a battalion of GI Joes, a squadron of superheroes, and loads of Legos.

The last gift was a shirt with an iron-on appliqué that read: "**Inside This Shirt Is One Terrific Kid!**" His eyes sparkled like the candles on his Superman cake as he examined his gift—stretching the neckline, peeking inside each armhole, and tugging open the bottom of the shirt. However, his smile quickly became a frown.

"Noah, why such a sad face?" I asked.

"Mommy, where's the kid?" Noah asked, offering me his shirt.

I realized that Noah literally thought a new pal was hiding inside his shirt. Of course, it made perfect sense to an Orange/Blue 6-year-old.

However, I knew that putting on his new shirt would erase his frustration. He wriggled into his shirt with his head and arms popping out like a little painted turtle. Then he posed as his favorite superhero, a mini-Superman, patting his chest with pride and exclaiming, "It's me!"

When I tell this story in my workshops, I never fail to hear "oh's" and "aww's." I use a replica of Noah's favorite childhood article of clothing because he wore his "It's me!" shirt until it became too small and threadbare.

Then I conclude the workshop with an invitation to the attendees to give themselves an "It's me!" gift, and I offer the same invitation to you.

Give yourself an "It's me!" gift each day. When you are deciding what to wear, be a kid and have fun. Transform yourself into a superhero! Imagine wearing a t-shirt underneath your clothing that complements your Brain Color. Begin the day knowing that inside your shirt is one terrific kid!

If you would like to change "terrific" to another adjective that describes you, please do. You might prefer creative, smart, organized, exciting, responsible, flexible, funny, competent, or courageous. If you are more comfortable changing "kid" to person, partner, parent, teacher, or friend, change that too.

I invite you to do what works best for you and your Brain Color. Enjoy celebrating your Brainday and yourself!

BIBLIOGRAPHY

Brizendine, L. (2006). *The female brain.* New York: Morgan Road Books.

Carter, R. (1999). *Mapping the mind.* Berkeley: University of California Press.

Emmett, R. (2005). *The clutter-busting handbook: Clean it up, clear it out, and keep your life clutter-free.* New York: Walker & Company.

Keirsey, D., & Bates, M. (1984). *Please understand me: Character and temperament types.* Del Mar, CA: Prometheus Nemesis.

Mellan, O. (1995). *Money harmony: Resolving money conflicts in your life and your relationships.* New York: Walker & Company.

Moire, A., & Jessel, D. (1992). *Brain sex: The real difference between men and women.* New York: Dell Publishing.

Tannen, D. (2001). *You just don't understand: Women and men in conversation.* New York: HarperCollins.

Warren, N. C. (1999). *How to know if someone is worth pursuing in two dates or less.* Nashville: Thomas Nelson.

OTHER BOOKS, CDS, AND DVDS YOU MIGHT ENJOY

Bell, A. H., & Smith, D. M. (2004). *Difficult people at work: How to cope, how to win.* New York: MJF Books.

Brinkman, R., & Kirschner, R. (2003). *Dealing with difficult people : 24 lessons for bringing out the best in everyone.* New York: McGraw Hill.

Campbell, C. O., & Campbell, G. O. (1995). *Views from a pier: Visions of hope, dreams, awareness, and peace.* Barrington, IL: PERQ Publications.

Campbell, J., & Cousineau, P. (1990). *The hero's journey: Joseph Campbell on his life and work.* New York: Harper & Row.

Balnicke J., & Kennard D (directors). (1988). *Joseph Campbell: The hero's journey* [documentary]. United States: Acadia.

Campbell, J., & Moyers, B. (1991). *The power of myth.* New York: Doubleday.

Chiazzari, S. (1998). *The complete book of color: Using color for lifestyle, health, and well-being.* Boston: Element.

Cline, F. W., & Fay, J. (1990). *Parenting with love and logic: Teaching children responsibility.* Colorado Springs: Pinon Press.

Conroy, E. (1921). *The symbolism of color.* London: Rider.

Diamant, A. (2003). *Pitching my tent: On marriage, motherhood, friendship, and other leaps of faith.* Parsippany, NJ: Simon & Schuster.

Emmett, R. (2000). *The procrastinator's handbook: Mastering the art of doing it now.* New York: Walker & Company.

Emmett, R. (2002). *The procrastinating child: A handbook for adults to help children stop putting things off.* New York: Walker & Company.

Eyre, L., & Eyre, R. (1993). *Teaching your children values.* Parsippany, NJ: Fireside.

Fontana, D. (2003). *The secret language of symbols: A visual key to symbols and their meanings.* San Francisco: Chronicle Books.

Foster, D. G., & Marshall, M. (1994). *How can I get through to you? Breakthrough communication beyond gender, beyond therapy, beyond deception.* New York: Hyperion.

Ginott, H. G. (1969). *Between parent and child.* New York: Avon Books.

Goodman, E., & O'Brien, P. (2001). *I know just what you mean: The power of friendship in women's lives.* Parsippany, NJ: Fireside.

Isay, J. (2007). *Walking on eggshells: Navigating the delicate relationship between adult children and parents.* New York: Flying Dolphin Press.

Jung, C. G. (1964). *Man and his symbols.* New York: Doubleday.

Keirsey, David. (1998). *Please understand me II: Temperament, character, intelligence.* Del Mar, CA: Prometheus Nemesis.

Kübler-Ross, E., & Kessler, D. (2000). *Life lessons: Two experts on death and dying teach us about the mysteries of life and living.* New York: Scribner.

Legato M. J. (2005). *Why men never remember and women never forget.* Emmaus, PA: Rodale.

Mellan, O. *Secret language of money* [CD]. Washington, DC: Olivia Mellan & Associates

Miller, M. *Brainstyles: Change your life without changing who you are.* New York: Simon & Schuster.

Moyers, B., Campbell, J., & Lucas, G. (1988). *Joseph Campbell and the power of myth* [documentary]. United States: Mystic Fire Video.

Myers Briggs, I. (1995). *Gifts differing: Understanding personality type.* Mountain View, CA: Davies-Black Publishing.

Nierenberg, G. I., & Calero, H. H. (2004). *How to read a person like a book.* New York: Barnes & Noble.

Pease, A., & Pease, B. (2001). *Why men don't listen and women can't read maps: How we're different and what to do about it.* New York: Broadway.

Roberts, C., & Roberts, S. (2001). *From this day forward.* New York: Harper Perennial.

Rossbach, S., & Yun, L. (1997). *Living color: Master Lin Yun's guide to Feng Shui and the art of color.* New York: Kodansha America.

Zichy, S. *Women and the Leadership Q: Revealing the Four Paths to Influence and Power.* New York: McGraw-Hill.

INDEX

A

ancient Egyptians, 14
ancient Greeks, 15
ancient Romans, 14, 15
appreciation, 14, 70
approval, 78
attitude, 55

B

balance, 56
behavior, 49, 108, 120, 126, 134
beliefs, 31
blend, 23
Blending Color, 22, 24, 25, 70
blue, 15
brain development, 77
brainbow, 21, 25–26
Briggs, Katharine Cook, *xv*
Brizendine, Louann, 69
Buddhist tradition, 15, 16
budget, 56

C

Carter, Rita, 4, 77
celebrations, 123–128, 139
challenge, 114
change, 16, 42, 111–114, 127, 128
    celebrating, 128
    environmental, 113–114
    family, 112
    life, 112–113
character, 13
characteristics, 50
children, 77–84, 93
Chinese tradition, 16
clarity, 121
Clouded Color, 22
Comfort Color, 22, 24, 25, 70
comfort level, 22
communication, 90, 93, 94, 106
compatibility, 106, 109
complementary, 21, 24, 26, 50
concern, 105
conflict, 21, 22, 23, 24, 106
conflict resolution, 105–109, 120, 139

confusion, 121
connecting, 97–103
contentment, 13
contrast, 21, 26, 50, 70
control, 54, 111
Convertible Color, 22, 25
cooperation, 60, 84
co-workers, 59–66, 92
creativity, 54, 82

D

De Berry, John, 128
decision making, 39, 117–121
differences, 13–18, 69
disappointment, 126, 127, 133
discomfort, 39
diversity, 17

E

emotions, 24, 92, 123, 126
energy, 16, 50, 82
environment, 42, 113–114
expectations, 125–126, 128

F

facts, 133
family, 69–75, 82, 93, 112, 127
focused, 82
Frank, Glenn, 36
friends, 69–75
frustration, 60, 125–126
fun, 26, 55, 84, 90, 126, 134, 139

G

gemstones, 7
gender, 69
gifts, 123, 125
green, 15

H

harmony, 21, 23, 60, 106
Henson, Jim, 13, 17
Hepburn, Katharine, 79
Hindu tradition, 15
holidays, 123–128
home, 49

I

ideal conditions, 39–44
impulsivity, 78
influence, 24
information, 15, 43, 49, 71, 126
intelligence, 99
intuition, 15, 111

J

Japanese tradition, 16
Jung, Carl, *xv*, 17, 89

K

Kiersey, David, 31
knowledge, 15

L

Lewis, C. S., 29
listening, 90, 93
logic, 24, 51, 78
Lorde, Audre, 69
love, 15, 16, 49–56, 71, 90, 91, 112, 118, 119, 125, 128, 132

M

Meevillain, 108
Mellan, Olivia, 55
memory, 15
misunderstandings, 13, 17, 59, 106, 108
Moir, Anne, 49
morale, 39
motivation, 31
Myers, Isabel Briggs, *xv*
Myers-Briggs Type Indicator (MBTI), *xv*

N

nature vs. nurture, 41–42
needs, 31
Newton, Sir Isaac, 21
Nhat Hanh, Thich, 105
Nin, Anaïs, 59

O

orange, 16
organized, 82, 83, 126
Owens, Bessie P., 75

P

Parachin, Victor, 128
peace, 15, 43, 120, 132
perception, 30, 49
personal life, 3–4
personality, 3, 7, 13, 17, 30, 42, 50, 98
perspective, 7–10, 26, 30, 31, 61, 111, 128
plan, 111
point of view (POV), 29–31, 36, 94, 108
prism, 21
privacy, 118
problem-solving, 15, 39
productivity, 60, 66
professional life, 3–4

R

rainbow, 21
rapport, 97–103
reality, 26
relationships, 91, 93, 97, 106, 133, 139
research, 120
respect, 13, 79
responsibility, 78, 97
risk, 25, 51, 97
risk-taking, 16, 26, 97, 113
romantic relationships, 49–56
rules, 14, 24, 97, 98, 134
Rushton, J. Philippe, 50

S

schedule, 91, 131, 132
self-confidence, 13, 16
self-esteem, 39
sensitivity, 17, 18, 98
Shadowed, 17–18, 22, 108
share, 50
solitude, 54
Sondheim, Stephen, 49
strengths, 7–10, 22, 24, 25, 31
stress, 117, 118, 128

T

talents, 26, 50, 54
Tannen, Deborah, 93
technology, 17
teenagers, 78–79
tension, 26
tolerance, 13
traditions, 123, 127, 128

U

understanding, 75, 93, 112

V

vacation, 70–71
values, 13, 31, 139
Venus, 15

W

Warren, Neil Clark, 50
work, 41, 59–66
worry, 132

Y

yellow, 14

AN INTERVIEW WITH THE AUTHOR

How did the idea for the WCIYB book come about?

The natural progression of my workshops and people asking me for WCIYB generated the idea to write the book. I believe writing a book is like falling in love—it happens when you are ready. The right time to write the words for this book arrived and I was ready!

Initially, WCIYB was an introductory mini-workshop for my strategic planning/creative problem-solving workshops. Because of my education, teaching experience, and professional development courses, I knew I could offer my clients another creative problem-solving technique that was easy and uncomplicated for adults and children.

Workshop participants enjoyed learning about the Brain Colors, and soon clients requested longer professional and personal development workshops. The more workshops I facilitated, the more people asked for a WCIYB book.

In 1997, I was inspired to write *Princess Shayna's Invisible Visible Gift*, which is WCIYB in a fairy-tale format for children. Working with the children, their parents, and teachers offered me more opportunities to facilitate workshops and presentations. The customized WCIYB work-books, all the data I compiled observing people's actions, listening to their conversations, and capturing ideas in a journal, on cocktail napkins, dining receipts, and scraps of paper became the research material I used to write WCIYB.

How have your previous professions prepared you for your current career?

My family exemplified and encouraged my tenacity, creativity, and adventurous spirit, which prepared me for my previous professions and career as an author.

I loved teaching elementary school, high school ESL, and creativity classes at several colleges and universities. I learned to recognize and understand different personality types and adapt to their learning styles in a variety of environments.

I was a student of customer safety and service when my husband and I owned and operated an aviation business (commuter airline, air ambulance, flight training, air charter and rental, ground and mainte-nance services) and managed the county airport in Mammoth Lakes, California.

As a professional speaker I have been privileged to work with a diverse group of clients in the U.S., Canada, Europe, and South America. They taught me about their fields of expertise, and I enjoyed teaching them how WCIYB could improve their organizations.

Each career has offered me opportunities to interact with and study each Brain Color, which has enriched my life and craft as a writer.

Which career would you say had the most influence on you?

Each of my careers has given me an abundance of lessons. However, I have always thought of myself as an educator. I feel my teaching experi-ences and relationships with my clients and students have influenced me the most.

I am an educator who loves gardening inside and outside the class-room. I enjoy planting seeds of knowledge, even though I may or may not have the joy of nurturing a seedling, watching it grow, and seeing the beauty of its blossom. However, I have had the pleasure of meeting former students and maintaining relationships with clients. It is encour-aging and joyful to learn how our experiences together have influenced their lives and mine.

This was true when I recognized one of my former students. He was a participant in a professional development workshop many years after he was a student in a third grade class I taught. My Blue heart sang when he realized who I was and told me he acquired his love for learning in my classroom.

From your perspective as a teacher, how do you think WCIYB can help children learn to get along better with their peers, parents, and teachers?

WCIYB teaches children the new 3 R's: Responsibility, Respect, and Relationships. Once, during a school visit, a sixth grader told me, "When you know your Brain Colors, you learn how to be responsible for the changes in your life and how to respect people who are different than you...be nice to other people, even when there are obstacles in your life."

Children and parents get along better with each other because they understand one another's Brain Colors and know how to speak BCSL— Brain Color as a Second Language. Recently, a friend shared his "Aha" with me: "For years I was perplexed because my child acted so differently from the rest of our family. Now, it all makes sense, I get it… he's Green."

WCIYB also helps children become responsible risk-takers vs. children at risk. They develop a healthy level of self-esteem, which makes them feel capable, worthy, in control, and empowered at school, at home, and in their communities. Several years ago, a reading specialist wrote about the impact WCIYB had on her students. She said, "The self-esteem lessons the children have learned are like peeling back the layers of an onion and enjoying the many layers. They really feel good about themselves and the real life skills they learned. The students speak from their hearts and their faces light up."

What are your favorite parts of sharing the WCIYB concept with different audiences?

I love sharing WCIYB with different audiences and knowing they have achieved their goals. Working with adult audiences, three of my favorite parts are:

- Enjoying the contagious laughter that fills a room after people discover their Brain Colors. They start comparing Brain Colors with the people around them. It's fun to hear: "No wonder we get along so well, we're exactly the same!"
- Listening to workshop participants begin to analyze their family members and friends. "I married a Yellow Brainer and have three Orange Brain children."
- Observing how quickly they transfer their Brain Colors from the workplace to their home. "I have to be Green at work, but I get to be Blue at home!"

Working with children, three of my favorite times have been:

- Watching the students come to class wearing a specific Brain Color tee shirt. "We're having a math test today, so I wore my Green Brainer shirt."
- Helping the children make a Brain Color/Princess Shayna patchwork quilt. I was surprised and honored when the class presented their quilt to me as a gift.
- Sharing Brain Color/Princess Shayna Celebrations with the students, their teachers, and their parents. In one classroom, we all enjoyed yellow pineapple pieces, blueberries, green grapes, and

orange slices while the children entertained us with their hilarious family Brain Color stories.

How can WCIYB help people achieve harmony in their home, between siblings, or between spouses?

To achieve harmony at home, I encourage adults and children to remember that *What Color Is Your Brain?* is an explanation, not an excuse for poor behavior. The following are two examples: "I'm not intruding on your Green privacy, I'm just being Blue" and "I'm Orange, so I don't have to follow your Yellow rules."

Family conflict is often the result of a common misconception. Adults and children think: "They are my family and they should automatically understand my behavior." Consequently, a "Soul Mate" can become a "Cell Mate" and "My Buddy" can become "The Bully." Recognizing the different Brain Colors helps family members resolve conflicts quickly and easily. Adults and children do not blame one another because they learn to understand the other person's perspective, strengths, values, needs, priorities, stress factors, and frustrations.

It takes time and effort to recognize, acknowledge, and appreciate other people's Brain Color attributes and abilities. However, when you do, you create a cooperative and comforting home environment with your siblings and spouse.

How can WCIYB help people improve their workplace environment?

If people utilize their Brain Colors to reduce stress, create ideal working conditions, and establish effective teamwork, they can improve their workplace environment.

Reducing stress by modifying office dynamics and diffusing problematic situations is easier when individuals know why they are compatible and incompatible with specific co-workers. The Brain Colors help them distinguish who are the "doubters" vs. the "doers" and the "talkers" vs. the "thinkers."

WCIYB can be utilized as an assessment for efficient job evaluation, staffing, and hiring to create ideal working conditions in which each Brain Color thrives. For example:

- Financial planners are Yellow Brainers who require job description manuals.
- Social workers are Blue Brainers who need genuine feedback.
- Technical consultants are Green Brainers who like systems and data.

- Sales professionals are Orange Brainers who want immediate results.

To build a successful business, it is beneficial to establish effective teams in a cooperative environment. Understanding how to connect with and motivate each team member is significant for success.

- A Yellow Brainer will be on time for meetings and help organize a plan.
- A Blue Brainer will encourage brainstorming and communicate ideas.
- A Green Brainer will develop an efficient strategy to execute the plan.
- An Orange Brainer will enthusiastically sell and get the results needed to be successful.

Implementing WCIYB will increase productivity, save time and money, and create a collaborative workplace environment.

Why are you allocating a percentage of the royalties from the sale of your book to the Juvenile Diabetes Research Foundation (JDRF)?

I am allocating 10% percent of the royalties to JDRF because of my commitment to help find a cure and offer comfort, education, and encouragement to children and their families who live with the challenges of diabetes.

I am not a researcher who works to find a cure for diabetes; however, I am a writer who writes the words that can offer financial support and create a greater awareness about diabetes.

I also want to honor and acknowledge our elder son, Joshua, who has Type I diabetes, my father who had Type II diabetes, and the millions of children, adults, and their families worldwide who deal with the daily "highs" and "lows" of diabetes.

About the Author

Sheila Glazov is an award-winning and internationally known author, personality type expert, professional speaker and educator. She earned her Bachelor of Science degree in education from the Ohio State University, a degree in Creative Leadership from Disney University, and is a graduate of the Creative Problem Solving Institute and the McNellis Creative Planning Institute. She has taught 3rd grade and High School ESL. Sheila has been an adjunct faculty member of William Rainey Harper College and a guest instructor at DePaul, Penn State, and Northwood Universities.

Sheila's education background, significant professional development and research opportunities enabled her to develop the **What Color Is Your Brain?® Workshop.** She is also the author of *Princess Shayna's Invisible Visible Gift* (www.PrincessShayna.com), which is the children's version of *What Color Is Your Brain?* She has facilitated her workshops in the U.S., Canada, Europe and South America with clients such as Motorola, Sears, CB Richard Ellis, Pulte Homes, TCF Bank, US Department of Labor, OSHA, New York Bar Association, Collaborative Law Institute, National Restaurant Association Education Foundation, Association of Occupational Health Professionals, Washoe Health System, Society of Women Engineers, National Association of Women Business Owners, Harvard Business School Club, Clemson University, Chicago Public Schools and Quest Academy. Encouraging adults and children to recognize and respect the best in themselves and others is the essence of her workshops and books.

Sheila's *What Color Is Your Brain?®* book and program incorporate a fun and fascinating approach to understanding yourself and others. Her personality color code helps individuals understand, value and accept their personality and the personalities of others, improve their job performance, communicate and collaborate more effectively, resolve conflicts quickly, build healthier relationships, and create harmony in their professional and personal lives.

Sheila has appeared on CNN, NBC, ABC, FOX, LIFETIME, and WGN TV. She has been interviewed on radio stations nationwide and featured in the *Wall Street Journal, Chicago Tribune, Chicago Sun Times,* and *Daily Herald* newspapers; *Selling Power, American Society of Training and Development, HR, Women's World, Seventeen,* and *Enterprising Women* magazines; and the Discover Card and Quill Corporation national customer newsletters. *Today's Chicago Woman* newspaper selected her as one of "100 Women Making A Difference".

Sheila's first book, **Princess Shayna's Invisible Visible Gift,** was published in 1997 and is the children's version of **What Color Is Your Brain?** Her educational and enchanting "Family Fairy Tale" offers children (ages 4-12) tools to recognize their Brain Color attributes and abilities to enhance their self-esteem and foster an appreciation of diversity. Ten percent of the royalties of Sheila's books is allocated to JDRF (Juvenile Diabetes Research Foundation).

Sheila has been a member of the National Speakers Association, National Speakers Association of Illinois, Governors' Commission on the Status of Women in Illinois, Congresswoman Melissa Bean's Women's Task Force, National Association of Women Business Owners, Women In Management, Women In Networking, Society of Children's Book Writers and Illustrators, International Women's Writer's Guild, National Association for Self-Esteem, and a variety of other associations, as well as a board member of many community organizations.

Sheila and her husband, Jordan, live in the Chicagoland area. To learn more about Sheila, her books and workshops, visit her website: www.sheilaglazov.com

---

The author will allocate 10% of the royalties from the sale of **What Color Is Your Brain?** to the Juvenile Diabetes Research Foundation (JDRF) to help her son, Joshua, and the other adults, children, and their families who deal with the challenges of diabetes.

Has the Brain Color concept impacted your life?

Share your fun and fascinating experience with family, friends, and coworkers. Order your copies today!

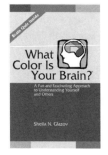

What Color Is Your Brain? A Fun and Fascinating Approach to Understanding Yourself and Others

Sheila N. Glazov

176 pp, Soft Cover, 2008, ISBN 10: 1-55642-807-3, ISBN 13: 978-1-55642-807-4, Order# 88073, $16.95

What Color Is Your Brain? explores the essential pieces of the puzzle that is human interaction, teaching us how to recognize and appreciate a spectrum of personality types. With the help of this dynamic book, discovering your own brain color and learning to adapt to others is bound to be a no-brainer.

"Everybody needs this book! An exciting and creative approach to understanding everyone's personality." — D.N. Evans, Fashion designer

www.whatcolorisyourbrain.com

Quantity	Title	Order #	Price
	What Color Is Your Brain? A Fun and Fascinating Approach to Understanding Yourself and Others	88073	$16.95

Are your shipping and billing addresses the same? ___yes ___no

Name: _____

Address: _____

City: _____ State: _____ Zip: _____

Phone: _____ Email: _____

_____ Check enclosed (Payable to SLACK Incorporated)

Charge my:

American Express _____ Visa _____ Mastercard_____

Account # _____

Exp date: _____ Security Code: _____

Signature: _____

Prices are subject to change without notice. Shipping charges may apply. Shipping and handling charges are non-refundable. Credit card orders will not be processed without security code.

Subtotal _____

Shipping _____

Handling $5.00

Sales Tax* _____

Total _____

Purchases in CA & NJ are subject to tax. Please add applicable state and local taxes.

SLACK Incorporated
Health Care Books and Journals
6900 Grove Road
Thorofare, NJ 08086
Call: 800-257-8290 or 856-848-1000
Fax: 856-848-6091
Visit: whatcolorisyourbrain.com
Email: orders@slackinc.com